The Primary

Ninja Foodi

Cookbook

UK 2023

365

Days of Fabulous and Facile Recipes
for You to Air Fry, Pressure Cook,
Slow Cook, Dehydrate and More on
Any Occasion

Portie K. Carter

Warning-Disclaimer

The purpose of this book is to educate and entertain. The author or publisher does not guarantee that anyone following the techniques, suggestions, tips, ideas, or strategies will become successful. The author and publisher shall have neither liability or responsibility to anyone with respect to any loss or damage caused, or alleged to be caused, directly or indirectly by the information contained in this book.

Table of Contents

Chapter 4 Poultry

Chapter 5 Fish and Seafood

Chapter 6 Beef, Pork, and Lamb

Chapter 7 Vegetables and Sides — 46

Chapter 8 Desserts — 54

INTRODUCTION

You may have seen the Ninja Foodi Max 9-in-1 Multi Cooker, Pressure Cooker, and Air Fryer advertised on TV or seen many users talk about it on TikTok. Maybe that spurred you to get one, or you saw them when shopping for a multi-purpose kitchen appliance.

The Ninja Foodi Pressure Cooker and Air Fryer are surprisingly popular and are the largest model in the Ninja Foodi multi-cooker family. It is perfect for health enthusiasts who want to enjoy fried chicken and chips without frying. It has more functionalities than other Ninja air fryers and multi cookers and is perfect for single meals. Once you have this, you may have to clear out all other single-use appliances from your kitchen countertop.

I was enticed to purchase it when I realized how much functionality it could dish out. I do a lot of batch cooking, but I majorly use it for cooking for two unless there are visitors. There was a time I had guests over, and I had to prepare food for five people. I quickly whipped out my Ninja Max and got to work, reducing my time in the kitchen.

Those with smaller kitchens may struggle with it, though, as it's quite large, but it's a perfect choice if you're trying to choose between an air fryer, slow cooker, and steamer but only have room for one. Sometimes, I ditch the hob and oven and simply use the Ninja Max; the results are always wonderful.

As much as I love using my Ninja Pressure Cooker and Air Fryer for most of my dinners, especially when I'm short on time, I have a couple of favuorites. My favourites are sourdough, casseroles, pasta bakes, chips, and freezer nibbles. These recipes and many more are all outlined in this cookbook.

You'd get to try that out with the recipes in this cookbook as you use your multipurpose kitchen appliance. The recipes in this cookbook have easy-to-source ingredients and very simple steps. As you can see, they involve a wide range of cooking methods, which is why you can expect to use this versatile kitchen appliance effectively.

Chapter 1 Basics of the Ninja Foodi Pressure Cooker & Air Fryer

Chapter 1 Basics of the Ninja Foodi Pressure Cooker & Air Fryer

The Ninja Foodi Max 9-in-1 Multi Cooker 7.5L, also called the Ninja Foodi Pressure Cooker and Air Fryer, is a multi-cooker that works with several kitchen appliances in one. It's first an air fryer that can cook food with less oil to give a crispy and crunchy finish. It also acts as an oven, pressure cooker, steamer, slow cooker, dehydrator, and grill. You can use it the same way you use your pot or pan without a hob.

How Does the Ninja Foodi Pressure Cooker & Air Fryer Work?

The Ninja Foodi Pressure Cooker and Air Fryer use TenderCrisp Technology to lock in juices and then crisp up food for a mouth-watering finish.

It comes with two lids, one built in for crisping, roasting, and cooking, including browning food. On the other hand, the secondary lid is for slow cooking and pressure cooking settings and is fitted to the appliance when the main lid is open. You can easily alternate between the pressure lid and the crisping lid to get perfect results for your food anytime you cook.

Its crisping lid allows food to be cooked with up to 75% less fat to give healthier alternatives, and its multi-functionality saves time in the kitchen.

The Ninja Max Multi Cooker is great for liquid-based dishes a typical air fryer can't cover, like sauce-heavy foods, and for foods that can only be prepared with a pressure cooker.

9-in-1 Versatility of the Ninja Foodi Pressure Cooker & Air Fryer

The Ninja Foodi Max Pressure Cooker and Air Fryer is a blessing for keen cooks who don't have much time to spend in the kitchen. It combines the following 9 functions and eliminates the need for several appliances on the kitchen countertop.

Pressure Cook

The pressure cook cuts cooking time by 70%, which is perfect for cooking meat while maintaining tenderness.

Air Crisp

This function gives food extra crispiness with little to no oil in the unit. You can enjoy chips, halloumi, or bread to toast.

Steam

The steam function saves the need for steaming baskets or appliances. It's perfect for steaming food quickly at high steam while maintaining nutrients. It works with the pressure cooker lid.

Slow Cook

It's perfect for cooking food at lower temperatures for long periods.

Yoghurt

Multicookers help with pasteurisng and fermenting milk for homemade yoghurt. You can use this function on low heat to get more yoghurt from live yoghurt and milk. It's a good buy instead of buying a special yoghurt maker.

Sear/Sauté

This setting is great for softening garlic and onions before adding the rest of the ingredients to the main pot for a casserole. There are different settings to choose from; low, low-medium, medium, medium-high, and high heat.

Bake/Roast

The bake function is a better alternative to putting the oven on high heat during the summer. The air crisp basket is great and specially designed for chicken wings. So, you can swap deep frying to air frying your chicken and other meals in the Ninja Foodi Max.

Grill

The air fry and grill functions are similar when cooking frozen food. However, the air fry function cooks frozen food bits faster.

Dehydrate

It's perfect for dehydrating orange, lemon, and lime slices for drinks and apples for healthy snacks.

Parts and Accessories

The Ninja Multi-Cooker has several parts which help increase its functionality. You can also obtain other accessories from Ninja for more stress-free cooking.

Pressure Lid

The Ninja Foodi is a pressure cooker and air fryer in one and so, comes with a separate pressure lid. It comes in handy for pressure cooking, slow cooking, and steaming and is not non-stick and ceramic coated. Since its removable, it can be stored in a drawer or cupboard alongside the racks when not in use. The pressure lid has an inscribed arrow and lock symbol to show you how to twist the lid

Crisping Lid

The crisping lid is attached to the cooker and can be opened anytime to check during the cooking process. Unlike the pressure lid, the crisping lid is ceramic-coated and non-stick and also dishwasher-safe. Anytime the lid is opened, the timer will pause, and the heating element will turn off. Immediately, it's covered, and the cooking process will continue with the timer resuming too.

Cooking Pot

This removable non-stick metal cooking pot has a large capacity of 7.6 liters, enough to feed up to six people. You can also purchase an extra cooking pot in cases where you're cooking a large meal and the other pot is full of delicacies already.

Cook and Crisp Basket

A crisper basket elevates food from the floor of the cooking basket so hot air can circulate it. The capacity and airflow design of the cook and crisp basket allows for air-crisping chicken wings and chips or for dehydrating fruits and meat.

The crisp basket in your Multi-Cooker is not your typical one. Aside from air crisping your food, it also allows you to pressure cook and steam. The ceramic-coated nonstick baskets are easy to clean, dishwasher safe, and PFAO free. The diffuser allows for all-round cooking and crisping.

The racks are reversible and perfect for steaming fish and vegetables. Immediately after placing water in the pot, you'd have to place the rack in and put your food on it, and then cover it with the pressure. These stainless steel reversible allows you to layer meat and proteins on top of vegetables and grains to enjoy complete one-pot meals. To properly steam delicate ingredients, simply reverse.

Care and Cleaning

Everything except the cooker are dishwater friendly. You can wash racks, crisper baskets, pots, pressure lids, and many accessories. The pots and baskets are non-stick, so they are easy to clean. If there is spillage, wipe immediately with a damp cloth.

The grills inside the main lid may be more challenging to clean, as they can get sticky with fat after using the air fryer. A great way to deal with that is to fill the pot with water and throw in a halved lemon. Let the lemon and water boil using the saute or slow cook function and turn it off with the lid closed, so the steam gets to work. Wipe with paper towels afterward.

A few cleaning tips for your Ninja Max 9-in-1 Multi Cooker:

♦ For a long-lasting kitchen appliance, it's best to clean after each use
♦ Ensure you unplug the unit from the wall socket before cleaning and take out al removable parts
♦ Clean removable parts with warm soapy water
♦ To clean the cooker base and control panel, use a damp cloth
♦ Air dry after each use
♦ Do not take apart the pressure release valve or float valve assembly when cleaning.
♦ To clean the crisping lid, wipe with a wet cloth or paper towel after it's cool.

Chapter 2 Breakfasts

Chapter 2 Breakfasts

Cheddar-Ham-Corn Muffins

Prep time: 10 minutes | Cook time: 6 to 8 minutes per batch | Makes 8 muffins

180 ml cornmeal/polenta	120 ml shredded sharp Cheddar cheese
60 ml flour	
1½ teaspoons baking powder	120 ml diced ham
¼ teaspoon salt	8 foil muffin cups, liners
1 egg, beaten	removed and sprayed with
2 tablespoons rapeseed oil	cooking spray
120 ml milk	

Preheat the Ninja Foodi Multi-cooker to 200ºC. In a medium bowl, stir together the cornmeal, flour, baking powder, and salt. Add egg, oil, and milk to dry ingredients and mix well. Stir in shredded cheese and diced ham. Divide batter among the muffin cups. Place 4 filled muffin cups in cook & crisp basket and bake for 5 minutes. Reduce temperature to 165ºC and bake for 1 to 2 minutes or until toothpick inserted in center of muffin comes out clean. Repeat steps 6 and 7 to cook remaining muffins.

Pumpkin Mug Muffin

Prep time: 5 minutes | Cook time: 9 minutes | Serves 1

120 ml sweetener	flour
120 ml blanched almond flour	1 egg
2 tablespoons organic pumpkin	1 tablespoon coconut oil
purée	½ teaspoon pumpkin pie spice
1 teaspoon sugar-free chocolate	½ teaspoon ground nutmeg
chips	½ teaspoon ground cinnamon
1 tablespoon organic coconut	⅛ teaspoon bicarbonate of soda

Mix the sweetener, almond flour, pumpkin purée, chocolate chips, coconut flour, egg, coconut oil, pumpkin pie spice, nutmeg, cinnamon, and bicarbonate of soda in a large bowl. Transfer this mixture into a well-greased, Ninja Foodi Multi-cooker-friendly mug. Pour 240 ml of filtered water into the inner pot of the Ninja Foodi Multi-cooker, and insert the trivet. Cover the mug in foil and place on top of the trivet. Close the lid, set the pressure release to Sealing. Set the Ninja Foodi Multi-cooker to 9 minutes on High Pressure. Once cooked, release the pressure immediately by switching the valve to Venting. Be sure your muffin is done by inserting a toothpick into the cake and making sure it comes out clean, as cook times may vary. Remove mug and enjoy!

Egg White Cups

Prep time: 10 minutes | Cook time: 15 minutes | Serves 4

475 ml 100% liquid egg whites	½ medium plum tomato, cored
3 tablespoons salted butter,	and diced
melted	120 ml chopped fresh spinach
¼ teaspoon salt	leaves
¼ teaspoon onion granules	

In a large bowl, whisk egg whites with butter, salt, and onion granules. Stir in tomato and spinach, then pour evenly into four ramekins greased with cooking spray. Place ramekins into cook & crisp basket. Adjust the temperature to 150ºC and bake for 15 minutes. Eggs will be fully cooked and firm in the center when done. Serve warm.

Bacon-and-Eggs Avocado

Prep time: 5 minutes | Cook time: 17 minutes | Serves 1

1 large egg	Fresh parsley, for serving
1 avocado, halved, peeled, and	(optional)
pitted	Sea salt flakes, for garnish
2 slices bacon	(optional)

Spray the cook & crisp basket with avocado oil. Preheat the Ninja Foodi Multi-cooker to 160ºC. Fill a small bowl with cool water. Soft-boil the egg: Place the egg in the cook & crisp basket. Air crisp for 6 minutes for a soft yolk or 7 minutes for a cooked yolk. Transfer the egg to the bowl of cool water and let sit for 2 minutes. Peel and set aside. Use a spoon to carve out extra space in the center of the avocado halves until the cavities are big enough to fit the soft-boiled egg. Place the soft-boiled egg in the center of one half of the avocado and replace the other half of the avocado on top, so the avocado appears whole on the outside. Starting at one end of the avocado, wrap the bacon around the avocado to completely cover it. Use toothpicks to hold the bacon in place. Place the bacon-wrapped avocado in the cook & crisp basket and air crisp for 5 minutes. Flip the avocado over and air crisp for another 5 minutes, or until the bacon is cooked to your liking. Serve on a bed of fresh parsley, if desired, and sprinkle with salt flakes, if desired. Best served fresh. Store extras in an airtight container in the fridge for up to 4 days. Reheat in a preheated 160ºC Ninja Foodi Multi-cooker for 4 minutes, or until heated through.

Cauliflower and Cheese Quiche

Prep time: 10 minutes | Cook time: 10 minutes | Serves 2

240 ml chopped cauliflower
60 ml shredded Cheddar cheese
5 eggs, beaten

1 teaspoon butter
1 teaspoon dried oregano
240 ml water

Grease the Ninja Foodi Multi-cooker baking pan with butter from inside. Pour water in the Ninja Foodi Multi-cooker. Sprinkle the cauliflower with dried oregano and put it in the prepared baking pan. Flatten the vegetables gently. After this, add eggs and stir the vegetables. Top the quiche with shredded cheese and transfer it in the Ninja Foodi Multi-cooker. Close and seal the lid. Cook the quiche on High Pressure for 10 minutes. Make a quick pressure release.

Simple Cinnamon Toasts

Prep time: 5 minutes | Cook time: 4 minutes | Serves 4

1 tablespoon salted butter
2 teaspoons ground cinnamon
4 tablespoons sugar

½ teaspoon vanilla extract
10 bread slices

Preheat the Ninja Foodi Multi-cooker to 190°C. In a bowl, combine the butter, cinnamon, sugar, and vanilla extract. Spread onto the slices of bread. Put the bread inside the Ninja Foodi Multi-cooker and bake for 4 minutes or until golden brown. Serve warm.

Smoky Sausage Patties

Prep time: 30 minutes | Cook time: 9 minutes | Serves 8

450 g pork mince
1 tablespoon soy sauce or tamari
1 teaspoon smoked paprika
1 teaspoon dried sage
1 teaspoon sea salt

½ teaspoon fennel seeds
½ teaspoon dried thyme
½ teaspoon freshly ground black pepper
¼ teaspoon cayenne pepper

In a large bowl, combine the pork, soy sauce, smoked paprika, sage, salt, fennel seeds, thyme, black pepper, and cayenne pepper. Work the meat with your hands until the seasonings are fully incorporated. Shape the mixture into 8 equal-size patties. Using your thumb, make a dent in the center of each patty. Place the patties on a plate and cover with plastic wrap. Refrigerate the patties for at least 30 minutes. Working in batches if necessary, place the patties in a single layer in the Ninja Foodi Multi-cooker, being careful not to overcrowd them. Set the Ninja Foodi Multi-cooker to 205°C and air crisp for 5 minutes. Flip and cook for about 4 minutes more.

Cinnamon-Raisin Bagels

Prep time: 30 minutes | Cook time: 10 minutes | Makes 4 bagels
Oil, for spraying
60 ml raisins
235 ml self-raising flour, plus more for dusting

235 ml plain Greek yoghurt
1 teaspoon ground cinnamon
1 large egg

Line the cook & crisp basket with parchment and spray lightly with oil. Place the raisins in a bowl of hot water and let sit for 10 to 15 minutes, until they have plumped. This will make them extra juicy. In a large bowl, mix together the flour, yoghurt, and cinnamon with your hands or a large silicone spatula until a ball is formed. It will be quite sticky for a while. Drain the raisins and gently work them into the ball of dough. Place the dough on a lightly floured work surface and divide into 4 equal pieces. Roll each piece into an 8- or 9-inch-long rope and shape it into a circle, pinching the ends together to seal. In a small bowl, whisk the egg. Brush the egg onto the tops of the dough. Place the dough in the prepared basket. Air crisp at 175°C for 10 minutes. Serve immediately.

Bacon and Spinach Eggs

Prep time: 5 minutes | Cook time: 9 minutes | Serves 4

2 tablespoons unsalted butter, divided
120 ml diced bacon
80 ml finely diced shallots
80 ml chopped spinach, leaves only
Pinch of sea salt

Pinch of black pepper
120 ml water
60 ml heavy whipping cream
8 large eggs
1 tablespoon chopped fresh chives, for garnish

Set the Ninja Foodi Multi-cooker on the Sauté mode and melt 1 tablespoon of the butter. Add the bacon to the pot and sauté for about 4 minutes, or until crispy. Using a slotted spoon, transfer the bacon bits to a bowl and set aside. Add the remaining 1 tablespoon of the butter and shallots to the pot and sauté for about 2 minutes, or until tender. Add the spinach leaves and sauté for 1 minute, or until wilted. Season with sea salt and black pepper and stir. Transfer the spinach to a separate bowl and set aside. Drain the oil from the pot into a bowl. Pour in the water and put the trivet inside. With a paper towel, coat four ramekins with the bacon grease. In each ramekin, place 1 tablespoon of the heavy whipping cream, reserved bacon bits and sautéed spinach. Crack two eggs without breaking the yolks in each ramekin. Cover the ramekins with aluminium foil. Place two ramekins on the trivet and stack the other two on top. Lock the lid. Set the cooking time for 2 minutes at Low Pressure. When the timer goes off, use a natural pressure release for 5 minutes, then release any remaining pressure. Carefully open the lid. Carefully take out the ramekins and serve garnished with the chives.

Minced Pork Breakfast Patties

Prep time: 5 minutes | Cook time: 15 minutes | Serves 4

450 g 84% lean minced pork	½ teaspoon salt
1 teaspoon dried thyme	¼ teaspoon pepper
½ teaspoon dried sage	¼ teaspoon red pepper flakes
½ teaspoon garlic powder	

Mix all ingredients in large bowl. Form into 4 patties based on preference. Press the Sauté button and press the Adjust button to lower heat to Less. Place patties in Ninja Foodi Multi-cooker and allow fat to render while patties begin browning. After 5 minutes, or when a few tablespoons of fat have rendered from meat, press the Start/Stop button. Press the Sauté button and press the Adjust button to set heat to Normal. Sear each side of patties and allow them to cook fully until no pink remains in centers, approximately 10 additional minutes, depending on thickness.

Hard-boiled Eggs

Prep time: 2 minutes | Cook time: 2 minutes | Serves 9

9 large eggs

Pour 240 ml of water into the electric pressure cooker and insert an egg rack. Gently stand the eggs in the rack, fat ends down. If you don't have an egg rack, place the eggs in a steamer basket or on a wire rack. Close and lock the lid of the pressure cooker. Set the valve to sealing. Cook on high pressure for 2 minutes. When the cooking is complete, hit Start/Stop and allow the pressure to release naturally. Once the pin drops, unlock and remove the lid. Using tongs, carefully remove the eggs from the pressure cooker. Peel or refrigerate the eggs when they are cool enough to handle.

Pecan and Walnut Granola

Prep time: 10 minutes | Cook time: 2 minutes | Serves 12

480 ml chopped raw pecans	120 ml slivered almonds
420 ml vanilla-flavored egg white protein powder	120 ml sesame seeds
	120 ml sweetener
300 ml unsalted butter, softened	1 teaspoon ground cinnamon
240 ml sunflower seeds	½ teaspoon sea salt
120 ml chopped raw walnuts	

Add all the ingredients to the Ninja Foodi Multi-cooker and stir to combine. Lock the lid, set the cooking time for 2 minutes on High Pressure. When the timer goes off, do a natural pressure release for 10 minutes, then release any remaining pressure. Open the lid. Stir well and pour the granola onto a sheet of baking paper to cool. It will become crispy when completely cool. Serve the granola in bowls.

Egg Tarts

Prep time: 10 minutes | Cook time: 17 to 20 minutes | Makes 2 tarts

⅓ sheet frozen puff pastry, thawed	2 eggs
	¼ teaspoon salt, divided
Cooking oil spray	1 teaspoon minced fresh parsley
120 ml shredded Cheddar cheese	(optional)

Preheat the Ninja Foodi Multi-cooker by selecting BAKE, setting the temperature to 200ºC, and setting the time to 3 minutes. Select START/STOP to begin. Lay the puff pastry sheet on a piece of parchment paper and cut it in half. Once the unit is preheated, spray the crisper plate with cooking oil. Transfer the 2 squares of pastry to the basket, keeping them on the parchment paper. Select BAKE, set the temperature to 200ºC, and set the time to 20 minutes. Select START/STOP to begin. After 10 minutes, use a metal spoon to press down the center of each pastry square to make a well. Divide the cheese equally between the baked pastries. Carefully crack an egg on top of the cheese, and sprinkle each with the salt. Resume cooking for 7 to 10 minutes. When the cooking is complete, the eggs will be cooked through. Sprinkle each with parsley (if using) and serve.

All-in-One Toast

Prep time: 10 minutes | Cook time: 10 minutes | Serves 1

1 strip bacon, diced	pepper, to taste
1 slice 1-inch thick bread	60 ml grated Monterey Jack or
1 egg	Chedday cheese
Salt and freshly ground black	

Preheat the Ninja Foodi Multi-cooker to 205ºC. Air crisp the bacon for 3 minutes, shaking the basket once or twice while it cooks. Remove the bacon to a paper towel lined plate and set aside. Use a sharp paring knife to score a large circle in the middle of the slice of bread, cutting halfway through, but not all the way through to the cutting board. Press down on the circle in the center of the bread slice to create an indentation. Transfer the slice of bread, hole side up, to the cook & crisp basket. Crack the egg into the center of the bread, and season with salt and pepper. Adjust the Ninja Foodi Multi-cooker temperature to 190ºC and air crisp for 5 minutes. Sprinkle the grated cheese around the edges of the bread, leaving the center of the yolk uncovered, and top with the cooked bacon. Press the cheese and bacon into the bread lightly to help anchor it to the bread and prevent it from blowing around in the Ninja Foodi Multi-cooker. Air crisp for one or two more minutes, just to melt the cheese and finish cooking the egg. Serve immediately.

Vegetable and Cheese Bake

Prep time: 7 minutes | Cook time: 9 minutes | Serves 3

3 eggs, beaten
60 ml coconut cream
¼ teaspoon salt
85 g Brussel sprouts, chopped
60 g tomato, chopped

85 g provolone cheese, shredded
1 teaspoon butter
1 teaspoon smoked paprika

Grease the Ninja Foodi Multi-cooker pan with the butter. Put eggs in the bowl, add salt, and smoked paprika. Whisk the eggs well. After this, add chopped Brussel sprouts and tomato. Pour the mixture into the Ninja Foodi Multi-cooker pan and sprinkle over with the shredded cheese. Pour 240 ml of the water in the Ninja Foodi Multi-cooker. Then place the pan with the egg mixture and close the lid. Cook the meal on High Pressure for 4 minutes. Then make naturally release for 5 minutes.

Pulled Pork Hash

Prep time: 10 minutes | Cook time: 15 minutes | Serves 4

4 eggs
280 g pulled pork, shredded
1 teaspoon coconut oil
1 teaspoon red pepper

1 teaspoon chopped fresh coriander
1 tomato, chopped
60 ml water

Melt the coconut oil in the Ninja Foodi Multi-cooker on Sauté mode. Then add pulled pork, red pepper, coriander, water, and chopped tomato. Cook the ingredients for 5 minutes. Then stir it well with the help of the spatula and crack the eggs over it. Close the lid. Cook the meal on High Pressure for 7 minutes. Then make a quick pressure release.

Classic Cinnamon Roll Coffee Cake

Prep time: 10 minutes | Cook time: 45 minutes | Serves 8

Cake:
480 ml almond flour
240 ml granulated sweetener
1 teaspoon baking powder
Pinch of salt
2 eggs
120 ml sour cream
4 tablespoons butter, melted
2 teaspoons vanilla extract

2 tablespoons sweetener
1½ teaspoons ground cinnamon
Cooking spray
120 ml water
Icing:
60 g cream cheese, softened
240 ml granulated sweetener
1 tablespoon double cream
½ teaspoon vanilla extract

In the bowl of a stand mixer, combine the almond flour, granulated sweetener, baking powder and salt. Mix until no lumps remain. Add the eggs, sour cream, butter and vanilla to the mixer bowl and mix until well combined. In a separate bowl, mix together the sweetener and cinnamon. Spritz the baking pan with cooking spray. Pour in the cake batter and use a knife to make sure it is level around the pan. Sprinkle the cinnamon mixture on top. Cover the pan tightly with aluminium foil. Pour the water and insert the trivet in the Ninja Foodi Multi-cooker. Put the pan on the trivet. Set the lid in place. Set the cooking time for 45 minutes on High Pressure. When the timer goes off, do a quick pressure release. Carefully open the lid. Remove the cake from the pot and remove the foil. Blot off any moisture on top of the cake with a paper towel, if necessary. Let rest in the pan for 5 minutes. Meanwhile, make the icing: In a small bowl, use a mixer to whip the cream cheese until it is light and fluffy. Slowly fold in the granulated sweetener and mix until well combined. Add the double cream and vanilla extract and mix until thoroughly combined. When the cake is cooled, transfer it to a platter and drizzle the icing all over.

Veggie Frittata

Prep time: 7 minutes | Cook time: 21 to 23 minutes | Serves 2

Avocado oil spray
60 ml diced red onion
60 ml diced red pepper
60 ml finely chopped broccoli
4 large eggs

85 g shredded sharp Cheddar cheese, divided
½ teaspoon dried thyme
Sea salt and freshly ground black pepper, to taste

Spray a pan well with oil. Put the onion, pepper, and broccoli in the pan, place the pan in the Ninja Foodi Multi-cooker, and set to 175ºC. Bake for 5 minutes. While the vegetables cook, beat the eggs in a medium bowl. Stir in half of the cheese, and season with the thyme, salt, and pepper. Add the eggs to the pan and top with the remaining cheese. Set the Ninja Foodi Multi-cooker to 175ºC. Bake for 16 to 18 minutes, until cooked through.

Red Pepper and Feta Frittata

Prep time: 10 minutes | Cook time: 20 minutes | Serves 4

Olive oil cooking spray
8 large eggs
1 medium red pepper, diced
½ teaspoon salt

½ teaspoon black pepper
1 garlic clove, minced
120 ml feta, divided

Preheat the Ninja Foodi Multi-cooker to 180ºC. Lightly coat the inside of a 6-inch round cake pan with olive oil cooking spray. In a large bowl, beat the eggs for 1 to 2 minutes, or until well combined. Add the red pepper, salt, black pepper, and garlic to the eggs, and mix together until the red pepper is distributed throughout. Fold in 60 ml the feta cheese. Pour the egg mixture into the prepared cake pan, and sprinkle the remaining 60 ml feta over the top. Place into the Ninja Foodi Multi-cooker and bake for 18 to 20 minutes, or until the eggs are set in the center. Remove from the Ninja Foodi Multi-cooker and allow to cool for 5 minutes before serving.

Cinnamon Roll Fat Bombs

Prep time: 5 minutes | Cook time: 5 minutes | Serves 5 to 6

2 tablespoons coconut oil

480 ml raw coconut butter

240 ml sugar-free chocolate chips

240 ml heavy whipping cream

120 ml sweetener, or more to taste

½ teaspoon ground cinnamon, or more to taste

½ teaspoon vanilla extract

Set the Ninja Foodi Multi-cooker to Sauté and melt the oil. Add the butter, chocolate chips, whipping cream, sweetener, cinnamon, and vanilla to the Ninja Foodi Multi-cooker and cook. Stir occasionally until the mixture reaches a smooth consistency. Pour mixture into a silicone mini-muffin mold. Freeze until firm. Serve, and enjoy!

Pizza Eggs

Prep time: 5 minutes | Cook time: 10 minutes | Serves 2

235 ml shredded Mozzarella cheese

7 slices pepperoni, chopped

1 large egg, whisked

¼ teaspoon dried oregano

¼ teaspoon dried parsley

¼ teaspoon garlic powder

¼ teaspoon salt

Place Mozzarella in a single layer on the bottom of an ungreased round nonstick baking dish. Scatter pepperoni over cheese, then pour egg evenly around baking dish. Sprinkle with remaining ingredients and place into cook & crisp basket. Adjust the temperature to 165°C and bake for 10 minutes. When cheese is brown and egg is set, dish will be done. Let cool in dish 5 minutes before serving.

Nutty "Oatmeal"

Prep time: 5 minutes | Cook time: 4 minutes | Serves 4

2 tablespoons coconut oil

240 ml full-fat coconut milk

240 ml heavy whipping cream

120 ml macadamia nuts

120 ml chopped pecans

80 ml sweetener, or more to taste

60 ml unsweetened coconut flakes

2 tablespoons chopped hazelnuts

2 tablespoons chia seeds

½ teaspoon ground cinnamon

Before you get started, soak the chia seeds for about 5 to 10 minutes (can be up to 20, if desired) in 240 ml of filtered water. After soaking, set the Ninja Foodi Multi-cooker to Sauté and add the coconut oil. Once melted, pour in the milk, whipping cream, and 240 ml of filtered water. Then add the macadamia nuts, pecans, sweetener, coconut flakes, hazelnuts, chia seeds, and cinnamon. Mix thoroughly inside the Ninja Foodi Multi-cooker. Close the lid, set the pressure release to Sealing, and hit Start/Stop to stop the current program. Set the Ninja Foodi Multi-cooker to 4 minutes on High Pressure, and let cook. Once cooked, carefully switch the pressure release to Venting. Open the Ninja Foodi Multi-cooker, serve, and enjoy!

Mini Chocolate Chip Muffins

Prep time: 5 minutes | Cook time: 20 minutes | Serves 7

240 ml blanched almond flour

2 eggs

180 ml sugar-free chocolate chips

1 tablespoon vanilla extract

120 ml sweetener, or more to

taste

2 tablespoons salted grass-fed butter, softened

½ teaspoon salt

¼ teaspoon bicarbonate of soda

Pour 240 ml of filtered water into the inner pot of the Ninja Foodi Multi-cooker, then insert the trivet. Using an electric mixer, combine flour, eggs, chocolate chips, vanilla, sweetener, butter, salt, and bicarbonate of soda. Mix thoroughly. Transfer this mixture into a well-greased Ninja Foodi Multi-cooker-friendly muffin (or egg bites) mold. Using a sling if desired, place the pan onto the trivet and cover loosely with aluminium foil. Close the lid, set the pressure release to Sealing. Set the Ninja Foodi Multi-cooker to 20 minutes on High Pressure and let cook. Once cooked, let the pressure naturally disperse from the Ninja Foodi Multi-cooker for about 10 minutes, then carefully switch the pressure release to Venting. Open the Ninja Foodi Multi-cooker and remove the pan. Let cool, serve, and enjoy!

Spinach and Swiss Frittata with Mushrooms

Prep time: 10 minutes | Cook time: 20 minutes | Serves 4

Olive oil cooking spray

8 large eggs

½ teaspoon salt

½ teaspoon black pepper

1 garlic clove, minced

475 ml fresh baby spinach

110 g baby mushrooms, sliced

1 shallot, diced

120 ml shredded Swiss cheese, divided

Hot sauce, for serving (optional)

Preheat the Ninja Foodi Multi-cooker to 180°C. Lightly coat the inside of a 6-inch round cake pan with olive oil cooking spray. In a large bowl, beat the eggs, salt, pepper, and garlic for 1 to 2 minutes, or until well combined. Fold in the spinach, mushrooms, shallot, and 60 ml the Swiss cheese. Pour the egg mixture into the prepared cake pan, and sprinkle the remaining 60 ml Swiss over the top. Place into the Ninja Foodi Multi-cooker and bake for 18 to 20 minutes, or until the eggs are set in the center. Remove from the Ninja Foodi Multi-cooker and allow to cool for 5 minutes. Drizzle with hot sauce (if using) before serving.

Portobello Eggs Benedict

Prep time: 10 minutes | Cook time: 10 to 14 minutes

| Serves 2

1 tablespoon olive oil	pepper, to taste
2 cloves garlic, minced	2 large eggs
¼ teaspoon dried thyme	2 tablespoons grated Pecorino
2 portobello mushrooms, stems	Romano cheese
removed and gills scraped out	1 tablespoon chopped fresh
2 plum tomatoes, halved	parsley, for garnish
lengthwise	1 teaspoon truffle oil (optional)
Salt and freshly ground black	

Preheat the Ninja Foodi Multi-cooker to 205ºC. In a small bowl, combine the olive oil, garlic, and thyme. Brush the mixture over the mushrooms and tomatoes until thoroughly coated. Season to taste with salt and freshly ground black pepper. Arrange the vegetables, cut side up, in the cook & crisp basket. Crack an egg into the center of each mushroom and sprinkle with cheese. Air crisp for 10 to 14 minutes until the vegetables are tender and the whites are firm. When cool enough to handle, coarsely chop the tomatoes and place on top of the eggs. Scatter parsley on top and drizzle with truffle oil, if desired, just before serving.

Spinach Omelet

Prep time: 5 minutes | Cook time: 12 minutes | Serves 2

4 large eggs	2 tablespoons salted butter,
350 ml chopped fresh spinach	melted
leaves	120 ml shredded mild Cheddar
2 tablespoons peeled and	cheese
chopped brown onion	¼ teaspoon salt

In an ungreased round nonstick baking dish, whisk eggs. Stir in spinach, onion, butter, Cheddar, and salt. Place dish into cook & crisp basket. Adjust the temperature to 160ºC and bake for 12 minutes. Omelet will be done when browned on the top and firm in the middle. Slice in half and serve warm on two medium plates.

Mozzarella Bacon Calzones

Prep time: 15 minutes | Cook time: 12 minutes | Serves 4

2 large eggs	60 g cream cheese, softened
235 ml blanched finely ground	and broken into small pieces
almond flour	4 slices cooked bacon,
475 ml shredded Mozzarella	crumbled
cheese	

Beat eggs in a small bowl. Pour into a medium nonstick skillet over medium heat and scramble. Set aside. In a large microwave-safe bowl, mix flour and Mozzarella. Add cream cheese to the bowl. Place bowl in microwave and cook 45 seconds on high to melt cheese, then stir with a fork until a soft dough ball forms. Cut a piece of parchment to fit cook & crisp basket. Separate dough into two sections and press each out into an 8-inch round. On half of each dough round, place half of the scrambled eggs and crumbled bacon. Fold the other side of the dough over and press to seal the edges. Place calzones on ungreased parchment and into cook & crisp basket. Adjust the temperature to 175ºC and set the timer for 12 minutes, turning calzones halfway through cooking. Crust will be golden and firm when done. Let calzones cool on a cooking rack 5 minutes before serving.

Keto Cabbage Hash Browns

Prep time: 5 minutes | Cook time: 8 minutes | Serves 3

240 ml shredded white cabbage	½ teaspoon onion powder
3 eggs, beaten	½ courgette, grated
½ teaspoon ground nutmeg	1 tablespoon coconut oil
½ teaspoon salt	

In a bowl, stir together all the ingredients, except for the coconut oil. Form the cabbage mixture into medium hash browns. Press the Sauté button on the Ninja Foodi Multi-cooker and heat the coconut oil. Place the hash browns in the hot coconut oil. Cook for 4 minutes on each side, or until lightly browned. Transfer the hash browns to a plate and serve warm.

Scotch Eggs

Prep time: 10 minutes | Cook time: 20 to 25 minutes

| Serves 4

2 tablespoons flour, plus extra	1 tablespoon water
for coating	Oil for misting or cooking spray
450 g sausage meat	Crumb Coating:
4 hard-boiled eggs, peeled	180 ml panko bread crumbs
1 raw egg	180 ml flour

Combine flour with sausage meat and mix thoroughly. Divide into 4 equal portions and mold each around a hard-boiled egg so the sausage completely covers the egg. In a small bowl, beat together the raw egg and water. Dip sausage-covered eggs in the remaining flour, then the egg mixture, then roll in the crumb coating. Air crisp at 180ºC for 10 minutes. Spray eggs, turn, and spray other side. Continue cooking for another 10 to 15 minutes or until sausage is well done.

Chapter 3 Snacks and Appetisers

Chapter 3 Snacks and Appetisers

Sweet Potato Fries with Mayonnaise

Prep time: 5 minutes | Cook time: 20 minutes | Serves 2 to 3

1 large sweet potato (about 450 g), scrubbed
1 teaspoon vegetable or rapeseed oil
Salt, to taste
Dipping Sauce:

60 ml light mayonnaise
½ teaspoon sriracha sauce
1 tablespoon spicy brown mustard
1 tablespoon sweet Thai chilli sauce

Preheat the Ninja Foodi Multi-cooker to 90ºC. On a flat work surface, cut the sweet potato into fry-shaped strips about ¼ inch wide and ¼ inch thick. You can use a mandoline to slice the sweet potato quickly and uniformly. In a medium bowl, drizzle the sweet potato strips with the oil and toss well. Transfer to the cook & crisp basket and air crisp for 10 minutes, shaking the basket twice during cooking. Remove the cook & crisp basket and sprinkle with the salt and toss to coat. Increase the Ninja Foodi Multi-cooker temperature to 205ºC and air crisp for an additional 10 minutes, or until the fries are crispy and tender. Shake the basket a few times during cooking. Meanwhile, whisk together all the ingredients for the sauce in a small bowl. Remove the sweet potato fries from the basket to a plate and serve warm alongside the dipping sauce.

Peppery Chicken Meatballs

Prep time: 5 minutes | Cook time: 13 to 20 minutes | Makes 16 meatballs

2 teaspoons olive oil
60 ml minced onion
60 ml minced red pepper
2 vanilla wafers, crushed

1 egg white
½ teaspoon dried thyme
230 g minced chicken breast

Preheat the Ninja Foodi Multi-cooker to 190ºC. In a baking pan, mix the olive oil, onion, and red pepper. Put the pan in the Ninja Foodi Multi-cooker. Air crisp for 3 to 5 minutes, or until the vegetables are tender. In a medium bowl, mix the cooked vegetables, crushed wafers, egg white, and thyme until well combined Mix in the chicken, gently but thoroughly, until everything is combined. Form the mixture into 16 meatballs and place them in the cook & crisp basket. Air crisp for 10 to 15 minutes, or until the meatballs reach an internal temperature of 75ºC on a meat thermometer. Serve immediately.

Rumaki

Prep time: 30 minutes | Cook time: 10 to 12 minutes per batch | Makes about 24 rumaki

283 g raw chicken livers
1 can sliced water chestnuts, drained

60 ml low-salt teriyaki sauce
12 slices turkey bacon

Cut livers into 1½-inch pieces, trimming out tough veins as you slice. Place livers, water chestnuts, and teriyaki sauce in small container with lid. If needed, add another tablespoon of teriyaki sauce to make sure livers are covered. Refrigerate for 1 hour. When ready to cook, cut bacon slices in half crosswise. Wrap 1 piece of liver and 1 slice of water chestnut in each bacon strip. Secure with toothpick. When you have wrapped half of the livers, place them in the cook & crisp basket in a single layer. Air crisp at 200ºC for 10 to 12 minutes, until liver is done, and bacon is crispy. While first batch cooks, wrap the remaining livers. Repeat step 6 to cook your second batch.

Polenta Fries with Chilli-Lime Mayo

Prep time: 10 minutes | Cook time: 28 minutes | Serves 4

Polenta Fries:
2 teaspoons vegetable or olive oil
¼ teaspoon paprika
450 g prepared polenta, cut into 3-inch × ½-inch strips
Chilli-Lime Mayo:
120 ml mayonnaise

1 teaspoon chilli powder
1 teaspoon chopped fresh coriander
¼ teaspoon ground cumin
Juice of ½ lime
Salt and freshly ground black pepper, to taste

Preheat the Ninja Foodi Multi-cooker to 205ºC. Mix the oil and paprika in a bowl. Add the polenta strips and toss until evenly coated. Transfer the polenta strips to the air crisp basket and air crisp for 28 minutes until the fries are golden brown, shaking the basket once during cooking. Season as desired with salt and pepper. Meanwhile, whisk together all the ingredients for the chilli-lime mayo in a small bowl. Remove the polenta fries from the Ninja Foodi Multi-cooker to a plate and serve alongside the chilli-lime mayo as a dipping sauce.

Bacon-Wrapped Shrimp and Jalapeño

Prep time: 20 minutes | Cook time: 26 minutes | Serves 8

24 large shrimp, peeled and deveined, about 340 g	divided
5 tablespoons barbecue sauce,	12 strips bacon, cut in half
	24 small pickled jalapeño slices

Toss together the shrimp and 3 tablespoons of the barbecue sauce. Let stand for 15 minutes. Soak 24 wooden toothpicks in water for 10 minutes. Wrap 1 piece bacon around the shrimp and jalapeño slice, then secure with a toothpick. Preheat the Ninja Foodi Multi-cooker to 175ºC. Working in batches, place half of the shrimp in the cook & crisp basket, spacing them ½ inch apart. Air crisp for 10 minutes. Turn shrimp over with tongs and air crisp for 3 minutes more, or until bacon is golden brown and shrimp are cooked through. Brush with the remaining barbecue sauce and serve.

Curried Broccoli Skewers

Prep time: 15 minutes | Cook time: 1 minute | Serves 2

240 ml broccoli florets	2 tablespoons coconut cream
½ teaspoon curry paste	240 ml water, for cooking

In the shallow bowl mix up curry paste and coconut cream. Then sprinkle the broccoli florets with curry paste mixture and string on the skewers. Pour water and insert the steamer rack in the Ninja Foodi Multi-cooker. Place the broccoli skewers on the rack. Close and seal the lid. Cook the meal on High Pressure for 1 minute. Make a quick pressure release.

Herbed Mushrooms

Prep time: 5 minutes | Cook time: 10 minutes | Serves 4

2 tablespoons butter	Sea salt, to taste
2 cloves garlic, minced	½ teaspoon freshly ground
570 g button mushrooms	black pepper
1 tablespoon coconut aminos	120 ml chicken broth
1 teaspoon dried rosemary	120 ml water
1 teaspoon dried basil	1 tablespoon roughly chopped
1 teaspoon dried sage	fresh parsley leaves, for garnish
1 bay leaf	

Set your Ninja Foodi Multi-cooker to Sauté and melt the butter. Add the garlic and mushrooms and sauté for 3 to 4 minutes until the garlic is fragrant. Add the remaining ingredients except the parsley to the Ninja Foodi Multi-cooker and stir well. Lock the lid. Set the cooking time for 5 minutes at High Pressure. When the timer beeps, perform a quick pressure release. Carefully open the lid. Remove the mushrooms from the pot to a platter. Serve garnished with the fresh parsley leaves.

Kale Chips with Sesame

Prep time: 15 minutes | Cook time: 8 minutes | Serves 5

2 L deribbed kale leaves, torn into 2-inch pieces	¼ teaspoon garlic powder
1½ tablespoons olive oil	½ teaspoon paprika
¾ teaspoon chilli powder	2 teaspoons sesame seeds

Preheat Ninja Foodi Multi-cooker to 175ºC. In a large bowl, toss the kale with the olive oil, chilli powder, garlic powder, paprika, and sesame seeds until well coated. Put the kale in the cook & crisp basket and air crisp for 8 minutes, flipping the kale twice during cooking, or until the kale is crispy. Serve warm.

Greek Yoghurt Devilled Eggs

Prep time: 15 minutes | Cook time: 15 minutes | Serves 4

4 eggs	⅛ teaspoon paprika
60 ml non-fat plain Greek yoghurt	⅛ teaspoon garlic powder
1 teaspoon chopped fresh dill	Chopped fresh parsley, for garnish
⅛ teaspoon salt	

Preheat the Ninja Foodi Multi-cooker to 130ºC. Place the eggs in a single layer in the cook & crisp basket and cook for 15 minutes. Quickly remove the eggs from the Ninja Foodi Multi-cooker and place them into a cold water bath. Let the eggs cool in the water for 10 minutes before removing and peeling them. After peeling the eggs, cut them in half. Spoon the yolk into a small bowl. Add the yoghurt, dill, salt, paprika, and garlic powder and mix until smooth. Spoon or pipe the yolk mixture into the halved egg whites. Serve with a sprinkle of fresh parsley on top.

Jalapeño Poppers

Prep time: 10 minutes | Cook time: 20 minutes | Serves 4

Oil, for spraying	parsley
227 g soft white cheese	½ teaspoon granulated garlic
177 ml gluten-free breadcrumbs, divided	½ teaspoon salt
2 tablespoons chopped fresh	10 jalapeño peppers, halved and seeded

Line the cook & crisp basket with parchment and spray lightly with oil. In a medium bowl, mix together the soft white cheese, half of the breadcrumbs, the parsley, garlic, and salt. Spoon the mixture into the jalapeño halves. Gently press the stuffed jalapeños in the remaining breadcrumbs. Place the stuffed jalapeños in the prepared basket. Air crisp at 190ºC for 20 minutes, or until the cheese is melted and the breadcrumbs are crisp and golden brown.

Rosemary-Garlic Shoestring Fries

Prep time: 5 minutes | Cook time: 18 minutes | Serves 2

1 large russet or Maris Piper potato (about 340 g), scrubbed clean, and julienned	rosemary
	Rock salt and freshly ground black pepper, to taste
1 tablespoon vegetable oil	1 garlic clove, thinly sliced
Leaves from 1 sprig fresh	Flaky sea salt, for serving

Preheat the Ninja Foodi Multi-cooker to 205°C. Place the julienned potatoes in a large colander and rinse under cold running water until the water runs clear. Spread the potatoes out on a double-thick layer of paper towels and pat dry. In a large bowl, combine the potatoes, oil, and rosemary. Season with rock salt and pepper and toss to coat evenly. Place the potatoes in the Ninja Foodi Multi-cooker and air crisp for 18 minutes, shaking the basket every 5 minutes and adding the garlic in the last 5 minutes of cooking, or until the fries are golden brown and crisp. Transfer the fries to a plate and sprinkle with flaky sea salt while they're hot. Serve immediately.

Veggie Salmon Nachos

Prep time: 10 minutes | Cook time: 9 to 12 minutes | Serves 6

57 g baked no-salt corn tortilla chips	1 red pepper, chopped
	120 ml grated carrot
1 (142 g) baked salmon fillet, flaked	1 jalapeño pepper, minced
	80 ml shredded low-salt low-fat Swiss cheese
120 ml canned low-salt black beans, rinsed and drained	1 tomato, chopped

Preheat the Ninja Foodi Multi-cooker to 180°C. In a baking pan, layer the tortilla chips. Top with the salmon, black beans, red pepper, carrot, jalapeño, and Swiss cheese. Bake in the Ninja Foodi Multi-cooker for 9 to 12 minutes, or until the cheese is melted and starts to brown. Top with the tomato and serve.

Creamy Mashed Cauliflower

Prep time: 3 minutes | Cook time: 1 minute | Serves 4

1 head cauliflower, chopped into florets	3 tablespoons butter
	2 tablespoons sour cream
240 ml water	½ teaspoon salt
1 clove garlic, finely minced	¼ teaspoon pepper

Place cauliflower on steamer rack. Add water and steamer rack to Ninja Foodi Multi-cooker. Press the Steam button and adjust time to 1 minute. When timer beeps, quick-release the pressure. Place cooked cauliflower into food processor and add remaining ingredients. Blend until smooth and creamy. Serve warm.

Buffalo Chicken Meatballs

Prep time: 5 minutes | Cook time: 10 minutes | Serves 4

450 g minced chicken	¼ teaspoon garlic powder
120 ml almond flour	240 ml water
2 tablespoons cream cheese	2 tablespoons butter, melted
1 packet dry ranch dressing mix	80 ml hot sauce
½ teaspoon salt	60 ml crumbled feta cheese
¼ teaspoon pepper	60 ml sliced spring onion

In large bowl, mix minced chicken, almond flour, cream cheese, ranch, salt, pepper, and garlic powder. Roll mixture into 16 balls. Place meatballs on steam rack and add 240 ml water to Ninja Foodi Multi-cooker. Click lid closed. Press the Meat/Stew button and set time for 10 minutes. Combine butter and hot sauce. When timer beeps, remove meatballs and place in clean large bowl. Toss in hot sauce mixture. Top with sprinkled feta and spring onions to serve.

Courgette and Cheese Tots

Prep time: 15 minutes | Cook time: 10 minutes | Serves 6

110 g Parmesan, grated	1 egg, beaten
110 g Cheddar cheese, grated	1 teaspoon dried oregano
1 courgette, grated	1 tablespoon coconut oil

In the mixing bowl, mix up Parmesan, Cheddar cheese, courgette, egg, and dried oregano. Make the small tots with the help of the fingertips. Then melt the coconut oil in the Ninja Foodi Multi-cooker on Sauté mode. Put the prepared courgette tots in the hot coconut oil and cook them for 3 minutes from each side or until they are light brown. Cool the courgette tots for 5 minutes.

Easy Spiced Nuts

Prep time: 5 minutes | Cook time: 25 minutes | Makes 3 L

1 egg white, lightly beaten	¼ teaspoon ground allspice
60 ml sugar	Pinch ground cayenne pepper
1 teaspoon salt	240 ml pecan halves
½ teaspoon ground cinnamon	240 ml cashews
¼ teaspoon ground cloves	240 ml almonds

Combine the egg white with the sugar and spices in a bowl. Preheat the Ninja Foodi Multi-cooker to 148°C. Spray or brush the cook & crisp basket with vegetable oil. Toss the nuts together in the spiced egg white and transfer the nuts to the cook & crisp basket. Air crisp for 25 minutes, stirring the nuts in the basket a few times during the cooking process. Taste the nuts (carefully because they will be very hot) to see if they are crunchy and nicely toasted. Air crisp for a few more minutes if necessary. Serve warm or cool to room temperature and store in an airtight container for up to two weeks.

Black Bean Corn Dip

Prep time: 10 minutes | Cook time: 10 minutes | Serves 4

½ (425 g) can black beans, drained and rinsed

½ (425 g) can corn, drained and rinsed

60 ml chunky salsa

57 g low-fat soft white cheese

60 ml shredded low-fat Cheddar cheese

½ teaspoon ground cumin

½ teaspoon paprika

Salt and freshly ground black pepper, to taste

Preheat the Ninja Foodi Multi-cooker to 165°C. In a medium bowl, mix together the black beans, corn, salsa, soft white cheese, Cheddar cheese, cumin, and paprika. Season with salt and pepper and stir until well combined. Spoon the mixture into a baking dish. Place baking dish in the cook & crisp basket and bake until heated through, about 10 minutes. Serve hot.

Lemon-Butter Mushrooms

Prep time: 10 minutes | Cook time: 4 minutes | Serves 2

240 ml cremini mushrooms, sliced

120 ml water

1 tablespoon lemon juice

1 teaspoon almond butter

1 teaspoon grated lemon zest

½ teaspoon salt

½ teaspoon dried thyme

Combine all the ingredients in the Ninja Foodi Multi-cooker. Secure the lid. Set the cooking time for 4 minutes at High Pressure. Once cooking is complete, do a natural pressure release for 5 minutes, then release any remaining pressure. Carefully open the lid. Serve warm.

Pickle Chips

Prep time: 30 minutes | Cook time: 12 minutes | Serves 4

Oil, for spraying

475 ml sliced dill or sweet pickles, drained

240 ml buttermilk

475 ml plain flour

2 large eggs, beaten

475 ml panko breadcrumbs

¼ teaspoon salt

Line the cook & crisp basket with parchment and spray lightly with oil. In a shallow bowl, combine the pickles and buttermilk and let soak for at least 1 hour, then drain. Place the flour, beaten eggs, and breadcrumbs in separate bowls. Coat each pickle chip lightly in the flour, dip in the eggs, and dredge in the breadcrumbs. Be sure each one is evenly coated. Place the pickle chips in the prepared basket, sprinkle with the salt, and spray lightly with oil. You may need to work in batches, depending on the size of your Ninja Foodi Multi-cooker. Air crisp at 200°C for 5 minutes, flip, and cook for another 5 to 7 minutes, or until crispy. Serve hot.

Rosemary Chicken Wings

Prep time: 10 minutes | Cook time: 16 minutes | Serves 4

4 boneless chicken wings

1 tablespoon olive oil

1 teaspoon dried rosemary

½ teaspoon garlic powder

¼ teaspoon salt

In the mixing bowl, mix up olive oil, dried rosemary, garlic powder, and salt. Then rub the chicken wings with the rosemary mixture and leave for 10 minutes to marinate. After this, put the chicken wings in the Ninja Foodi Multi-cooker, add the remaining rosemary marinade and cook them on Sauté mode for 8 minutes from each side.

Sausage Balls with Cheese

Prep time: 10 minutes | Cook time: 10 to 11 minutes | Serves 8

340 g mild sausage meat

355 ml baking mix

240 ml shredded mild Cheddar cheese

85 g soft white cheese, at room temperature

1 to 2 tablespoons olive oil

Preheat the Ninja Foodi Multi-cooker to 165°C. Line the cook & crisp basket with parchment paper. Mix together the ground sausage, baking mix, Cheddar cheese, and soft white cheese in a large bowl and stir to incorporate. Divide the sausage mixture into 16 equal portions and roll them into 1-inch balls with your hands. Arrange the sausage balls on the parchment, leaving space between each ball. You may need to work in batches to avoid overcrowding. Brush the sausage balls with the olive oil. Bake for 10 to 11 minutes, shaking the basket halfway through, or until the balls are firm and lightly browned on both sides. Remove from the basket to a plate and repeat with the remaining balls. Serve warm.

Herbed Courgette Slices

Prep time: 5 minutes | Cook time: 5 minutes | Serves 4

2 tablespoons olive oil

2 garlic cloves, chopped

450 g courgette, sliced

120 ml water

120 ml sugar-free tomato purée

1 teaspoon dried thyme

½ teaspoon dried rosemary

½ teaspoon dried oregano

Set your Ninja Foodi Multi-cooker to Sauté and heat the olive oil. Add the garlic and sauté for 2 minutes until fragrant. Add the remaining ingredients to the Ninja Foodi Multi-cooker and stir well. Lock the lid. Set the cooking time for 3 minutes at Low Pressure. When the timer beeps, perform a quick pressure release. Carefully remove the lid. Serve warm.

Cheese Drops

Prep time: 15 minutes | Cook time: 10 minutes per batch | Serves 8

177 ml plain flour
½ teaspoon rock salt
¼ teaspoon cayenne pepper
¼ teaspoon smoked paprika
¼ teaspoon black pepper
Dash garlic powder (optional)

60 ml butter, softened
240 ml shredded extra mature Cheddar cheese, at room temperature
Olive oil spray

In a small bowl, combine the flour, salt, cayenne, paprika, pepper, and garlic powder, if using. Using a food processor, cream the butter and cheese until smooth. Gently add the seasoned flour and process until the dough is well combined, smooth, and no longer sticky. (Or make the dough in a stand mixer fitted with the paddle attachment: Cream the butter and cheese on medium speed until smooth, then add the seasoned flour and beat at low speed until smooth.) Divide the dough into 32 equal-size pieces. On a lightly floured surface, roll each piece into a small ball. Spray the cook & crisp basket with oil spray. Arrange 16 cheese drops in the basket. Set the Ninja Foodi Multi-cooker to 165ºC for 10 minutes, or until drops are just starting to brown. Transfer to a wire rack. Repeat with remaining dough, checking for doneness at 8 minutes. Cool the cheese drops completely on the wire rack. Store in an airtight container until ready to serve, or up to 1 or 2 days.

Courgette Fries with Roasted Garlic Aioli

Prep time: 20 minutes | Cook time: 12 minutes | Serves 4

1 tablespoon vegetable oil
½ head green or savoy cabbage, finely shredded
Roasted Garlic Aioli:
1 teaspoon roasted garlic
120 ml mayonnaise
2 tablespoons olive oil
Juice of ½ lemon
Salt and pepper, to taste

Courgette Fries:
120 ml flour
2 eggs, beaten
240 ml seasoned breadcrumbs
Salt and pepper, to taste
1 large courgette, cut into ½-inch sticks
Olive oil

Make the aioli: Combine the roasted garlic, mayonnaise, olive oil and lemon juice in a bowl and whisk well. Season the aioli with salt and pepper to taste. Prepare the courgette fries. Create a dredging station with three shallow dishes. Place the flour in the first shallow dish and season well with salt and freshly ground black pepper. Put the beaten eggs in the second shallow dish. In the third shallow dish, combine the breadcrumbs, salt and pepper. Dredge the courgette sticks, coating with flour first, then dipping them into the eggs to coat, and finally tossing in breadcrumbs. Shake the dish with the breadcrumbs and pat the crumbs onto the courgette sticks gently with your hands, so they stick evenly. Place the courgette fries on a flat surface and let them sit at least 10 minutes before air crisping to let them dry out a little. Preheat the Ninja Foodi Multi-cooker to 205ºC. Spray the courgette sticks with olive oil and place them into the cook & crisp basket. You can air crisp the courgette in two layers, placing the second layer in the opposite direction to the first. Air crisp for 12 minutes turning and rotating the fries halfway through the cooking time. Spray with additional oil when you turn them over. Serve courgette fries warm with the roasted garlic aioli.

Chilli-Brined Fried Calamari

Prep time: 20 minutes | Cook time: 8 minutes | Serves 2

1 (227 g) jar sweet or hot pickled cherry peppers
227 g calamari bodies and tentacles, bodies cut into ½-inch-wide rings
1 lemon
475 ml plain flour
Rock salt and freshly ground

black pepper, to taste
3 large eggs, lightly beaten
Cooking spray
120 ml mayonnaise
1 teaspoon finely chopped rosemary
1 garlic clove, minced

Drain the pickled pepper brine into a large bowl and tear the peppers into bite-size strips. Add the pepper strips and calamari to the brine and let stand in the refrigerator for 20 minutes or up to 2 hours. Grate the lemon zest into a large bowl then whisk in the flour and season with salt and pepper. Dip the calamari and pepper strips in the egg, then toss them in the flour mixture until fully coated. Spray the calamari and peppers liberally with cooking spray, then transfer half to the Ninja Foodi Multi-cooker. Air crisp at 205ºC, shaking the basket halfway into cooking, until the calamari is cooked through and golden brown, about 8 minutes. Transfer to a plate and repeat with the remaining pieces. In a small bowl, whisk together the mayonnaise, rosemary, and garlic. Squeeze half the zested lemon to get 1 tablespoon of juice and stir it into the sauce. Season with salt and pepper. Cut the remaining zested lemon half into 4 small wedges and serve alongside the calamari, peppers, and sauce.

Creamy Spinach

Prep time: 5 minutes | Cook time: 4 minutes | Serves 4

480 ml chopped spinach
60 g Monterey Jack cheese, shredded
240 ml almond milk

1 tablespoon butter
1 teaspoon minced garlic
½ teaspoon salt

Combine all the ingredients in the Ninja Foodi Multi-cooker. Secure the lid. Set the cooking time for 4 minutes at High Pressure. Once cooking is complete, do a quick pressure release. Carefully open the lid. Give the mixture a good stir and serve warm.

Italian Tomatillos

Prep time: 10 minutes | Cook time: 10 minutes | Serves 4

1 tablespoon Italian seasoning
4 tomatillos, sliced

4 teaspoons olive oil
4 tablespoons water

Sprinkle the tomatillos with Italian seasoning. Then pour the olive oil in the Ninja Foodi Multi-cooker and heat it up on Sauté mode for 1 minute. Put the tomatillos in the Ninja Foodi Multi-cooker in one layer and cook them for 2 minutes from each side. Then add water and close the lid. Sauté the vegetables for 3 minutes more.

Stuffed Jalapeños with Bacon

Prep time: 10 minutes | Cook time: 6 minutes | Serves 2

30 g bacon, chopped, fried
60 g Cheddar cheese, shredded
1 tablespoon coconut cream

1 teaspoon chopped spring onions
2 jalapeños, trimmed and seeded

Mix together the chopped bacon, cheese, coconut cream, and spring onions in a mixing bowl and stir until well incorporated. Stuff the jalapeños evenly with the bacon mixture. Press the Sauté button to heat your Ninja Foodi Multi-cooker. Place the stuffed jalapeños in the Ninja Foodi Multi-cooker and cook each side for 3 minutes until softened. Transfer to a paper towel-lined plate and serve.

Spinach and Crab Meat Cups

Prep time: 10 minutes | Cook time: 10 minutes | Makes 30 cups

1 (170 g) can crab meat, drained to yield 80 ml meat
60 ml frozen spinach, thawed, drained, and chopped
1 clove garlic, minced
120 ml grated Parmesan cheese
3 tablespoons plain yoghurt

¼ teaspoon lemon juice
½ teaspoon Worcestershire sauce
30 mini frozen filo shells, thawed
Cooking spray

Preheat the Ninja Foodi Multi-cooker to 200°C. Remove any bits of shell that might remain in the crab meat. Mix the crab meat, spinach, garlic, and cheese together. Stir in the yoghurt, lemon juice, and Worcestershire sauce and mix well. Spoon a teaspoon of filling into each filo shell. Spray the cook & crisp basket with cooking spray and arrange half the shells in the basket. Air crisp for 5 minutes. Repeat with the remaining shells. Serve immediately.

Chapter 4 Poultry

Chapter 4 Poultry

Broccoli Chicken Divan

Prep time: 15 minutes | Cook time: 10 minutes | Serves 4

240 ml chopped broccoli	60 ml chicken broth
2 tablespoons cream cheese	120 ml grated Cheddar cheese
120 ml double cream	170 g chicken fillet, cooked and
1 tablespoon curry powder	chopped

Mix up broccoli and curry powder and put the mixture in the Ninja Foodi Multi-cooker. Add double cream and cream cheese. Then add chicken and mix up the ingredients. Then add chicken broth and double cream. Top the mixture with Cheddar cheese. Close and seal the lid. Cook the meal on High Pressure for 10 minutes. Allow the natural pressure release for 5 minutes, open the lid and cool the meal for 10 minutes.

Easy Cajun Chicken Drumsticks

Prep time: 5 minutes | Cook time: 40 minutes | Serves 5

1 tablespoon olive oil	seasoning
10 chicken drumsticks	Salt and ground black pepper,
1½ tablespoons Cajun	to taste

Preheat the Ninja Foodi Multi-cooker to 200ºC. Grease the cook & crisp basket with olive oil. On a clean work surface, rub the chicken drumsticks with Cajun seasoning, salt, and ground black pepper. Arrange the seasoned chicken drumsticks in a single layer in the Ninja Foodi Multi-cooker. You need to work in batches to avoid overcrowding. Air crisp for 18 minutes or until lightly browned. Flip the drumsticks halfway through. Remove the chicken drumsticks from the Ninja Foodi Multi-cooker. Serve immediately.

Pesto Chicken

Prep time: 5 minutes | Cook time: 25 minutes | Serves 2

2 (170 g) boneless, skinless	240 ml water
chicken breasts, butterflied	60 ml whole-milk ricotta cheese
½ teaspoon salt	60 ml pesto
¼ teaspoon pepper	60 ml shredded whole-milk
¼ teaspoon dried parsley	Mozzarella cheese
¼ teaspoon garlic powder	Chopped parsley, for garnish
2 tablespoons coconut oil	(optional)

Sprinkle the chicken breasts with salt, pepper, parsley, and garlic powder. Set your Ninja Foodi Multi-cooker to Sauté and melt the coconut oil. Add the chicken and brown for 3 to 5 minutes. Remove the chicken from the pot to a 1.8 L glass bowl. Pour the water into the Ninja Foodi Multi-cooker and use a wooden spoon or rubber spatula to make sure no seasoning is stuck to bottom of pot. Scatter the ricotta cheese on top of the chicken. Pour the pesto over chicken, and sprinkle the Mozzarella cheese over chicken. Cover with aluminium foil. Add the trivet to the Ninja Foodi Multi-cooker and place the bowl on the trivet. Secure the lid. Set the cooking time for 20 minutes at High Pressure. Once cooking is complete, do a natural pressure release for 10 minutes, then release any remaining pressure. Carefully open the lid. Serve the chicken garnished with the chopped parsley, if desired.

Broccoli Cheese Chicken

Prep time: 15 minutes | Cook time: 25 minutes | Serves 4

1 tablespoon avocado oil	additional for seasoning,
15 g chopped onion	divided
35 g finely chopped broccoli	¼ freshly ground black pepper,
115 g cream cheese, at room	plus additional for seasoning,
temperature	divided
60 g Cheddar cheese, shredded	900 g boneless, skinless chicken
1 teaspoon garlic powder	breasts
½ teaspoon sea salt, plus	1 teaspoon smoked paprika

Heat a medium skillet over medium-high heat and pour in the avocado oil. Add the onion and broccoli and cook, stirring occasionally, for 5 to 8 minutes, until the onion is tender. Transfer to a large bowl and stir in the cream cheese, Cheddar cheese, and garlic powder, and season to taste with salt and pepper. Hold a sharp knife parallel to the chicken breast and cut a long pocket into one side. Stuff the chicken pockets with the broccoli mixture, using toothpicks to secure the pockets around the filling. In a small dish, combine the paprika, ½ teaspoon salt, and ¼ teaspoon pepper. Sprinkle this over the outside of the chicken. Set the Ninja Foodi Multi-cooker to 200ºC. Place the chicken in a single layer in the cook & crisp basket, cooking in batches if necessary, and cook for 14 to 16 minutes, until an instant-read thermometer reads 70ºC. Place the chicken on a plate and tent a piece of aluminum foil over the chicken. Allow to rest for 5 to 10 minutes before serving.

Chicken Escabèche

Prep time: 5 minutes | Cook time: 15 minutes | Serves 4

240 ml filtered water
450 g chicken, mixed pieces
3 garlic cloves, smashed
2 bay leaves
1 onion, chopped
120 ml red wine vinegar
½ teaspoon coriander
½ teaspoon ground cumin
½ teaspoon mint, finely chopped
½ teaspoon rock salt
½ teaspoon freshly ground black pepper

Pour the water into the Ninja Foodi Multi-cooker and insert the trivet. Thoroughly combine the chicken, garlic, bay leaves, onion, vinegar, coriander, cumin, mint, salt, and black pepper in a large bowl. Put the bowl on the trivet and cover loosely with aluminium foil. Secure the lid. Set the cooking time for 15 minutes at High Pressure. Once cooking is complete, do a natural pressure release for 10 minutes, then release any remaining pressure. Carefully open the lid. Remove the dish from the Ninja Foodi Multi-cooker and cool for 5 to 10 minutes before serving.

Thanksgiving Turkey

Prep time: 5 minutes | Cook time: 60 minutes | Serves 8

1 turkey breast (3.2 kg), giblets removed
4 tablespoons butter, softened
2 teaspoons ground sage
2 teaspoons garlic powder
2 teaspoons salt
2 teaspoons black pepper
½ onion, quartered
1 rib celery, cut into 3 or 4 pieces
240 ml chicken broth
2 or 3 bay leaves
1 teaspoon xanthan gum

Pat the turkey dry with a paper towel. In a small bowl, combine the butter with the sage, garlic powder, salt, and pepper. Rub the butter mixture all over the top of the bird. Place the onion and celery inside the cavity. Place the trivet in the pot. Add the broth and bay leaves to the pot. Place the turkey on the trivet. If you need to remove the trivet to make the turkey fit, you can. The turkey will be near the top of the pot, which is fine. Close the lid and seal the vent. Cook on High Pressure for 35 minutes. It is normal if it takes your pot a longer time to come to pressure. Let the steam naturally release for 20 minutes before Manually releasing. Press Start/Stop. Heat the broiler. Carefully remove the turkey to a baking tray. Place under the broiler for 5 to 10 minutes to crisp up the skin. While the skin is crisping, use the juices to make a gravy. Pour the juices through a mesh sieve, reserving 480 ml of broth. Return the reserved broth to the pot. Turn the pot to Sauté mode. When the broth starts to boil, add the xanthan gum and whisk until the desired consistency is reached. Add more xanthan gum if you like a thicker gravy. Remove the turkey from the broiler and place on a platter. Carve as desired and serve with the gravy.

Wild Rice and Kale Stuffed Chicken Thighs

Prep time: 10 minutes | Cook time: 22 minutes | Serves 4

4 boneless, skinless chicken thighs
250 g cooked wild rice
35 g chopped kale
2 garlic cloves, minced
1 teaspoon salt
Juice of 1 lemon
100 g crumbled feta
Olive oil cooking spray
1 tablespoon olive oi

Preheat the Ninja Foodi Multi-cooker to 190°C. Place the chicken thighs between two pieces of plastic wrap, and using a meat mallet or a rolling pin, pound them out to about ¼-inch thick. In a medium bowl, combine the rice, kale, garlic, salt, and lemon juice and mix well. Place a quarter of the rice mixture into the middle of each chicken thigh, then sprinkle 2 tablespoons of feta over the filling. Spray the cook & crisp basket with olive oil cooking spray. Fold the sides of the chicken thigh over the filling, and then gently place each of them seam-side down into the cook & crisp basket. Brush each stuffed chicken thigh with olive oil. Roast the stuffed chicken thighs for 12 minutes, then turn them over and cook for an additional 10 minutes, or until the internal temperature reaches 75°C.

Fried Chicken Breasts

Prep time: 30 minutes | Cook time: 12 to 14 minutes | Serves 4

450 g boneless, skinless chicken breasts
180 ml dill pickle juice
70 g finely ground blanched almond flour
70 g finely grated Parmesan
cheese
½ teaspoon sea salt
½ teaspoon freshly ground black pepper
2 large eggs
Avocado oil spray

Place the chicken breasts in a zip-top bag or between two pieces of plastic wrap. Using a meat mallet or heavy skillet, pound the chicken to a uniform ½-inch thickness. Place the chicken in a large bowl with the pickle juice. Cover and allow to brine in the refrigerator for up to 2 hours. In a shallow dish, combine the almond flour, Parmesan cheese, salt, and pepper. In a separate, shallow bowl, beat the eggs. Drain the chicken and pat it dry with paper towels. Dip in the eggs and then in the flour mixture, making sure to press the coating into the chicken. Spray both sides of the coated breasts with oil. Spray the cook & crisp basket with oil and put the chicken inside. Set the temperature to 200°C and air crisp for 6 to 7 minutes. Carefully flip the breasts with a spatula. Spray the breasts again with oil and continue cooking for 6 to 7 minutes more, until golden and crispy.

Chicken Legs with Leeks

Prep time: 30 minutes | Cook time: 18 minutes | Serves 6

2 leeks, sliced
2 large-sized tomatoes, chopped
3 cloves garlic, minced
½ teaspoon dried oregano
6 chicken legs, boneless and

skinless
½ teaspoon smoked cayenne
pepper
2 tablespoons olive oil
A freshly ground nutmeg

In a mixing dish, thoroughly combine all ingredients, minus the leeks. Place in the refrigerator and let it marinate overnight. Lay the leeks onto the bottom of the cook & crisp basket. Top with the chicken legs. Roast chicken legs at (190ºC for 18 minutes, turning halfway through. Serve with hoisin sauce.

Fajita Chicken Strips

Prep time: 10 minutes | Cook time: 15 minutes | Serves 4

450 g boneless, skinless chicken
tenderloins, cut into strips
3 bell peppers, any color, cut
into chunks
1 onion, cut into chunks

1 tablespoon olive oil
1 tablespoon fajita seasoning
mix
Cooking spray

Preheat the Ninja Foodi Multi-cooker to 190ºC. In a large bowl, mix together the chicken, bell peppers, onion, olive oil, and fajita seasoning mix until completely coated. Spray the cook & crisp basket lightly with cooking spray. Place the chicken and vegetables in the cook & crisp basket and lightly spray with cooking spray. Air crisp for 7 minutes. Shake the basket and air crisp for an additional 5 to 8 minutes, until the chicken is cooked through and the veggies are starting to char. Serve warm.

Chicken Schnitzel

Prep time: 15 minutes | Cook time: 5 minutes | Serves 4

60 g all-purpose flour
1 teaspoon marjoram
½ teaspoon thyme
1 teaspoon dried parsley flakes
½ teaspoon salt
1 egg

1 teaspoon lemon juice
1 teaspoon water
120 g breadcrumbs
4 chicken tenders, pounded
thin, cut in half lengthwise
Cooking spray

Preheat the Ninja Foodi Multi-cooker to 200ºC and spritz with cooking spray. Combine the flour, marjoram, thyme, parsley, and salt in a shallow dish. Stir to mix well. Whisk the egg with lemon juice and water in a large bowl. Pour the breadcrumbs in a separate shallow dish. Roll the chicken halves in the flour mixture first, then in the egg mixture, and then roll over the breadcrumbs to coat well. Shake the excess off. Arrange the chicken halves in the preheated Ninja Foodi Multi-cooker and spritz with cooking spray

on both sides. Air crisp for 5 minutes or until the chicken halves are golden brown and crispy. Flip the halves halfway through. Serve immediately.

Chicken Pesto Pizzas

Prep time: 10 minutes | Cook time: 12 minutes | Serves 4

450 g chicken mince thighs
¼ teaspoon salt
⅛ teaspoon ground black
pepper

20 g basil pesto
225 g shredded Mozzarella
cheese
4 grape tomatoes, sliced

Cut four squares of parchment paper to fit into your cook & crisp basket. Place chicken mince in a large bowl and mix with salt and pepper. Divide mixture into four equal sections. Wet your hands with water to prevent sticking, then press each section into a 6-inch circle onto a piece of ungreased parchment. Place each chicken crust into cook & crisp basket, working in batches if needed. Adjust the temperature to 180ºC and air crisp for 10 minutes, turning crusts halfway through cooking. Spread 1 tablespoon pesto across the top of each crust, then sprinkle with ¼ of the Mozzarella and top with 1 sliced tomato. Continue cooking at 180ºC for 2 minutes. Cheese will be melted and brown when done. Serve warm.

Chicken and Vegetable Fajitas

Prep time: 15 minutes | Cook time: 23 minutes | Serves 6

Chicken:
450 g boneless, skinless chicken
thighs, cut crosswise into thirds
1 tablespoon vegetable oil
4½ teaspoons taco seasoning
Vegetables:
50 g sliced onion
150 g sliced bell pepper
1 or 2 jalapeños, quartered
lengthwise

1 tablespoon vegetable oil
½ teaspoon kosher salt
½ teaspoon ground cumin
For Serving:
Tortillas
Sour cream
Shredded cheese
Guacamole
Salsa

For the chicken: In a medium bowl, toss together the chicken, vegetable oil, and taco seasoning to coat. For the vegetables: In a separate bowl, toss together the onion, bell pepper, jalapeño(s), vegetable oil, salt, and cumin to coat. Place the chicken in the cook & crisp basket. Set the Ninja Foodi Multi-cooker to (190ºC for 10 minutes. Add the vegetables to the basket, toss everything together to blend the seasonings, and set the Ninja Foodi Multi-cooker for 13 minutes more. Use a meat thermometer to ensure the chicken has reached an internal temperature of 75ºC. Transfer the chicken and vegetables to a serving platter. Serve with tortillas and the desired fajita fixings.

BLT Chicken Salad

Prep time: 15 minutes | Cook time: 17 minutes | Serves 4

4 slices bacon

2 (170 g) chicken breasts

1 teaspoon salt

½ teaspoon garlic powder

¼ teaspoon dried parsley

¼ teaspoon pepper

¼ teaspoon dried thyme

240 ml water

480 ml chopped romaine lettuce

Sauce:

80 ml mayonnaise

30 g chopped pecans

120 ml diced plum tomatoes

½ avocado, diced

1 tablespoon lemon juice

Press the Sauté button to heat your Ninja Foodi Multi-cooker. Add the bacon and cook for about 7 minutes, flipping occasionally, until crisp. Remove and place on a paper towel to drain. When cool enough to handle, crumble the bacon and set aside. Sprinkle the chicken with salt, garlic powder, parsley, pepper, and thyme. Pour the water into the Ninja Foodi Multi-cooker. Use a wooden spoon to ensure nothing is stuck to the bottom of the pot. Add the trivet to the pot and place the chicken on top of the trivet. Secure the lid. Set the cooking time for 10 minutes at High Pressure. Meanwhile, whisk together all the ingredients for the sauce in a large salad bowl. Once cooking is complete, do a quick pressure release. Carefully open the lid. Remove the chicken and let sit for 10 minutes. Cut the chicken into cubes and transfer to the salad bowl, along with the cooked bacon. Gently stir until the chicken is thoroughly coated. Mix in the lettuce right before serving.

Chicken Paillard

Prep time: 10 minutes | Cook time: 10 minutes | Serves 2

2 large eggs, room temperature

1 tablespoon water

40 g powdered Parmesan cheese or pork dust

2 teaspoons dried thyme leaves

1 teaspoon ground black pepper

2 (140 g) boneless, skinless chicken breasts, pounded to ½ inch thick

Lemon Butter Sauce:

2 tablespoons unsalted butter, melted

2 teaspoons lemon juice

¼ teaspoon finely chopped fresh thyme leaves, plus more for garnish

⅛ teaspoon fine sea salt

Lemon slices, for serving

Spray the cook & crisp basket with avocado oil. Preheat the Ninja Foodi Multi-cooker to 200°C. Beat the eggs in a shallow dish, then add the water and stir well. In a separate shallow dish, mix together the Parmesan, thyme, and pepper until well combined. One at a time, dip the chicken breasts in the eggs and let any excess drip off, then dredge both sides of the chicken in the Parmesan mixture. As you finish, set the coated chicken in the cook & crisp basket. Roast the chicken in the Ninja Foodi Multi-cooker for 5 minutes, then flip the chicken and cook for another 5 minutes, or until cooked through and the internal temperature reaches 75°C. While the chicken cooks, make the lemon butter sauce: In a small bowl, mix together

all the sauce ingredients until well combined. Plate the chicken and pour the sauce over it. Garnish with chopped fresh thyme and serve with lemon slices. Store leftovers in an airtight container in the refrigerator for up to 4 days. Reheat in a preheated 200°C Ninja Foodi Multi-cooker for 5 minutes, or until heated through.

Classic Whole Chicken

Prep time: 5 minutes | Cook time: 50 minutes | Serves 4

Oil, for spraying

1 (1.8 kg) whole chicken, giblets removed

1 tablespoon olive oil

1 teaspoon paprika

½ teaspoon granulated garlic

½ teaspoon salt

½ teaspoon freshly ground black pepper

¼ teaspoon finely chopped fresh parsley, for garnish

Line the cook & crisp basket with parchment and spray lightly with oil. Pat the chicken dry with paper towels. Rub it with the olive oil until evenly coated. In a small bowl, mix together the paprika, garlic, salt, and black pepper and sprinkle it evenly over the chicken. Place the chicken in the prepared basket, breast-side down. Air crisp at 180°C for 30 minutes, flip, and cook for another 20 minutes, or until the internal temperature reaches 75°C and the juices run clear. Sprinkle with the parsley before serving.

Stuffed Chicken with Spinach and Feta

Prep time: 10 minutes | Cook time: 25 minutes | Serves 4

120 ml frozen spinach

80 ml crumbled feta cheese

1¼ teaspoons salt, divided

4 (170 g) boneless, skinless chicken breasts, butterflied

¼ teaspoon pepper

¼ teaspoon dried oregano

¼ teaspoon dried parsley

¼ teaspoon garlic powder

2 tablespoons coconut oil

240 ml water

Combine the spinach, feta cheese, and ¼ teaspoon of salt in a medium bowl. Divide the mixture evenly and spoon onto the chicken breasts. Close the chicken breasts and secure with toothpicks or butcher's string. Sprinkle the chicken with the remaining 1 teaspoon of salt, pepper, oregano, parsley, and garlic powder. Set your Ninja Foodi Multi-cooker to Sauté and heat the coconut oil. Sear each chicken breast until golden brown, about 4 to 5 minutes per side. Remove the chicken breasts and set aside. Pour the water into the Ninja Foodi Multi-cooker and scrape the bottom to remove any chicken or seasoning that is stuck on. Add the trivet to the Ninja Foodi Multi-cooker and place the chicken on the trivet. Secure the lid. Set the cooking time for 15 minutes at High Pressure. Once cooking is complete, do a natural pressure release for 15 minutes, then release any remaining pressure. Carefully open the lid. Serve warm.

Barbecue Chicken and Coleslaw Tostadas

Prep time: 15 minutes | Cook time: 40 minutes |
Makes 4 tostadas

Coleslaw:	pepper
60 g sour cream	Tostadas:
25 g small green cabbage, finely chopped	280 g pulled rotisserie chicken
½ tablespoon white vinegar	120 ml barbecue sauce
½ teaspoon garlic powder	4 corn tortillas
½ teaspoon salt	110 g shredded Mozzarella cheese
¼ teaspoon ground black	Cooking spray

Make the Coleslaw: Combine the ingredients for the coleslaw in a large bowl. Toss to mix well. Refrigerate until ready to serve. Make the Tostadas: Preheat the Ninja Foodi Multi-cooker to 190ºC. Spritz the cook & crisp basket with cooking spray. Toss the chicken with barbecue sauce in a separate large bowl to combine well. Set aside. Place one tortilla in the preheated Ninja Foodi Multi-cooker and spritz with cooking spray. Work in batches to avoid overcrowding. Air crisp the tortilla for 5 minutes or until lightly browned, then spread a quarter of the barbecue chicken and cheese over. Air crisp for another 5 minutes or until the cheese melts. Repeat with remaining tortillas, chicken, and cheese. Serve the tostadas with coleslaw on top.

African Chicken Peanut Stew

Prep time: 10 minutes | Cook time: 10 minutes | Serves 6

240 ml chopped onion	1 tablespoon sugar-free tomato paste
2 tablespoons minced garlic	
1 tablespoon minced fresh ginger	450 g boneless, skinless chicken breasts or thighs, cut into large chunks
1 teaspoon salt	
½ teaspoon ground cumin	720 ml - 1 L chopped Swiss chard
½ teaspoon ground coriander	
½ teaspoon freshly ground black pepper	240 ml cubed raw pumpkin
½ teaspoon ground cinnamon	120 ml water
⅛ teaspoon ground cloves	240 ml chunky peanut butter

In the inner cooking pot of the Ninja Foodi Multi-cooker, stir together the onion, garlic, ginger, salt, cumin, coriander, pepper, cinnamon, cloves, and tomato paste. Add the chicken, chard, pumpkin, and water. Lock the lid into place. Adjust the pressure to High. Cook for 10 minutes. When the cooking is complete, let the pressure release naturally. Unlock the lid. Mix in the peanut butter a little at a time. Taste with each addition, as your reward for cooking. The final sauce should be thick enough to coat the back of a spoon in a thin layer. Serve over mashed cauliflower, cooked courgette noodles, steamed vegetables, or with a side salad.

Thai Curry Meatballs

Prep time: 10 minutes | Cook time: 10 minutes | Serves 4

450 g chicken mince	1 tablespoon fish sauce
15 g chopped fresh coriander	2 garlic cloves, minced
1 teaspoon chopped fresh mint	2 teaspoons minced fresh ginger
1 tablespoon fresh lime juice	½ teaspoon kosher salt
1 tablespoon Thai red, green, or yellow curry paste	½ teaspoon black pepper
	¼ teaspoon red pepper flakes

Preheat the Ninja Foodi Multi-cooker to 200ºC. In a large bowl, gently mix the chicken mince, coriander, mint, lime juice, curry paste, fish sauce, garlic, ginger, salt, black pepper, and red pepper flakes until thoroughly combined. Form the mixture into 16 meatballs. Place the meatballs in a single layer in the cook & crisp basket. Air crisp for 10 minutes, turning the meatballs halfway through the cooking time. Use a meat thermometer to ensure the meatballs have reached an internal temperature of 75ºC. Serve immediately.

Korean Flavour Glazed Chicken Wings

Prep time: 10 minutes | Cook time: 25 minutes | Serves 4

Wings:	1 tablespoon minced garlic
900 g chicken wings	1 teaspoon agave nectar
1 teaspoon salt	2 packets Splenda
1 teaspoon ground black pepper	1 tablespoon sesame oil
Sauce:	For Garnish:
2 tablespoons gochujang	2 teaspoons sesame seeds
1 tablespoon mayonnaise	15 g chopped green onions
1 tablespoon minced ginger	

Preheat the Ninja Foodi Multi-cooker to 200ºC. Line a baking pan with aluminum foil, then arrange the rack on the pan. On a clean work surface, rub the chicken wings with salt and ground black pepper, then arrange the seasoned wings on the rack. Air crisp for 20 minutes or until the wings are well browned. Flip the wings halfway through. You may need to work in batches to avoid overcrowding. Meanwhile, combine the ingredients for the sauce in a small bowl. Stir to mix well. Reserve half of the sauce in a separate bowl until ready to serve. Remove the air fried chicken wings from the Ninja Foodi Multi-cooker and toss with remaining half of the sauce to coat well. Place the wings back to the Ninja Foodi Multi-cooker and air crisp for 5 more minutes or until the internal temperature of the wings reaches at least 75ºC. Remove the wings from the Ninja Foodi Multi-cooker and place on a large plate. Sprinkle with sesame seeds and green onions. Serve with reserved sauce.

Parmesan Carbonara Chicken

Prep time: 15 minutes | Cook time: 25 minutes | Serves 5

450 g chicken, skinless, boneless, chopped	60 g Parmesan, grated
240 ml double cream	1 teaspoon ground black pepper
240 ml chopped spinach	1 tablespoon coconut oil
	60 g bacon, chopped

Put the coconut oil and chopped chicken in the Ninja Foodi Multi-cooker. Sauté the chicken for 10 minutes. Stir it from time to time. Then add ground black pepper, and spinach. Stir the mixture well and sauté for 5 minutes more. Then add double cream and Parmesan. Close and seal the lid. Cook the meal on High Pressure for 10 minutes. Allow the natural pressure release for 10 minutes.

Sesame Chicken with Broccoli

Prep time: 15 minutes | Cook time: 12 minutes | Serves 2

½ teaspoon five spices	120 ml chicken broth
½ teaspoon sesame seeds	1 teaspoon coconut aminos
120 ml chopped broccoli	1 tablespoon avocado oil
170 g chicken fillet, sliced	

In the mixing bowl, mix up avocado oil, coconut aminos, and sesame seeds. Add five spices. After this, mix up sliced chicken fillet and coconut aminos mixture. Put the chicken in the Ninja Foodi Multi-cooker. Add chicken broth and broccoli. Close and seal the lid. Cook the meal on High Pressure for 12 minutes. Make a quick pressure release.

Marjoram Chicken Wings with Cream Cheese

Prep time: 7 minutes | Cook time: 10 minutes | Serves 2

1 teaspoon marjoram	pepper
1 teaspoon cream cheese	400 g chicken wings
½ green pepper	180 ml water
½ teaspoon salt	1 teaspoon coconut oil
½ teaspoon ground black	

Rub the chicken wings with the marjoram, salt, and ground black pepper. Blend the green pepper until you get a purée. Rub the chicken wings in the green pepper purée. Then toss the coconut oil in the Ninja Foodi Multi-cooker bowl and preheat it on the Sauté mode. Add the chicken wings and cook them for 3 minutes from each side or until light brown. Then add cream cheese and water. Cook the meal for 4 minutes at High Pressure. When the time is over, make a quick pressure release. Let the cooked chicken wings chill for 1 to 2 minutes and serve them!

Chicken Hand Pies

Prep time: 30 minutes | Cook time: 10 minutes per batch | Makes 8 pies

180 ml chicken broth	1 tablespoon milk
130 g frozen mixed peas and carrots	Salt and pepper, to taste
140 g cooked chicken, chopped	1 (8-count) can organic flaky biscuits
1 tablespoon cornflour	Oil for misting or cooking spray

In a medium saucepan, bring chicken broth to a boil. Stir in the frozen peas and carrots and cook for 5 minutes over medium heat. Stir in chicken. Mix the cornflour into the milk until it dissolves. Stir it into the simmering chicken broth mixture and cook just until thickened. Remove from heat, add salt and pepper to taste, and let cool slightly. Lay biscuits out on wax paper. Peel each biscuit apart in the middle to make 2 rounds so you have 16 rounds total. Using your hands or a rolling pin, flatten each biscuit round slightly to make it larger and thinner. Divide chicken filling among 8 of the biscuit rounds. Place remaining biscuit rounds on top and press edges all around. Use the tines of a fork to crimp biscuit edges and make sure they are sealed well. Spray both sides lightly with oil or cooking spray. Cook in a single layer, 4 at a time, at 170ºC for 10 minutes or until biscuit dough is cooked through and golden brown.

Chili Lime Turkey Burgers

Prep time: 10 minutes | Cook time: 3 minutes | Serves 4

Burgers:	Juice and zest of 1 lime
900 g minced turkey	120 ml water
45 g diced red onion	Dipping Sauce:
2 cloves garlic, minced	120 ml sour cream
1½ teaspoons minced coriander	4 teaspoons sriracha
1½ teaspoons salt	1 tablespoon chopped coriander, plus more for garnish
1 teaspoon Mexican chili powder	1 teaspoon lime juice

Make the burgers: In a large bowl, add the turkey, onion, garlic, coriander, salt, chili powder, and lime juice and zest. Use a wooden spoon to mix until the ingredients are well distributed. Divide the meat into four 230-g balls. Use a kitchen scale to measure for accuracy. Pat the meat into thick patties, about 1 inch thick. Add the water and trivet to the Ninja Foodi Multi-cooker. Place the turkey patties on top of the trivet, overlapping if necessary. Close the lid and seal the vent. Cook on High Pressure for 3 minutes. Quick release the steam. Remove the patties from the pot. Make the dipping sauce: In a small bowl, whisk together the sour cream, sriracha, coriander, and lime juice. Top each patty with 2 tablespoons of the sauce and garnish with fresh coriander.

Pecan-Crusted Chicken Tenders

Prep time: 10 minutes | Cook time: 12 minutes | Serves 4

2 tablespoons mayonnaise
1 teaspoon Dijon mustard
455 g boneless, skinless chicken tenders
½ teaspoon salt

¼ teaspoon ground black pepper
75 g chopped roasted pecans, finely ground

In a small bowl, whisk mayonnaise and mustard until combined. Brush mixture onto chicken tenders on both sides, then sprinkle tenders with salt and pepper. Place pecans in a medium bowl and press each tender into pecans to coat each side. Place tenders into ungreased cook & crisp basket in a single layer, working in batches if needed. Adjust the temperature to (190ºC and roast for 12 minutes, turning tenders halfway through cooking. Tenders will be golden brown and have an internal temperature of at least 75ºC when done. Serve warm.

African Merguez Meatballs

Prep time: 30 minutes | Cook time: 10 minutes | Serves 4

450 g chicken mince
2 garlic cloves, finely minced
1 tablespoon sweet Hungarian paprika
1 teaspoon kosher salt
1 teaspoon sugar

1 teaspoon ground cumin
½ teaspoon black pepper
½ teaspoon ground fennel
½ teaspoon ground coriander
½ teaspoon cayenne pepper
¼ teaspoon ground allspice

In a large bowl, gently mix the chicken, garlic, paprika, salt, sugar, cumin, black pepper, fennel, coriander, cayenne, and allspice until all the ingredients are incorporated. Let stand for 30 minutes at room temperature, or cover and refrigerate for up to 24 hours. Form the mixture into 16 meatballs. Arrange them in a single layer in the cook & crisp basket. Set the Ninja Foodi Multi-cooker to 200ºC for 10 minutes, turning the meatballs halfway through the cooking time. Use a meat thermometer to ensure the meatballs have reached an internal temperature of 75ºC.

Herb-Buttermilk Chicken Breast

Prep time: 5 minutes | Cook time: 40 minutes | Serves 2

1 large bone-in, skin-on chicken breast
240 ml buttermilk
1½ teaspoons dried parsley
1½ teaspoons dried chives
¾ teaspoon kosher salt

½ teaspoon dried dill
½ teaspoon onion powder
¼ teaspoon garlic powder
¼ teaspoon dried tarragon
Cooking spray

Place the chicken breast in a bowl and pour over the buttermilk, turning the chicken in it to make sure it's completely covered. Let the chicken stand at room temperature for at least 20 minutes or in the refrigerator for up to 4 hours. Meanwhile, in a bowl, stir together the parsley, chives, salt, dill, onion powder, garlic powder, and tarragon. Preheat the Ninja Foodi Multi-cooker to 150ºC. Remove the chicken from the buttermilk, letting the excess drip off, then place the chicken skin-side up directly in the Ninja Foodi Multi-cooker. Sprinkle the seasoning mix all over the top of the chicken breast, then let stand until the herb mix soaks into the buttermilk, at least 5 minutes. Spray the top of the chicken with cooking spray. Bake for 10 minutes, then increase the temperature to 180ºC and bake until an instant-read thermometer inserted into the thickest part of the breast reads 80ºC and the chicken is deep golden brown, 30 to 35 minutes. Transfer the chicken breast to a cutting board, let rest for 10 minutes, then cut the meat off the bone and cut into thick slices for serving.

Authentic Chicken Shawarma

Prep time: 15 minutes | Cook time: 17 minutes | Serves 4

450 g chicken fillet
½ teaspoon ground coriander
½ teaspoon smoked paprika
½ teaspoon dried thyme

1 tablespoon tahini sauce
1 teaspoon lemon juice
1 teaspoon double cream
240 ml water, for cooking

Rub the chicken fillet with ground coriander, smoked paprika, thyme, and wrap in the foil. Then pour water and insert the steamer rack in the Ninja Foodi Multi-cooker. Place the wrapped chicken in the steamer; close and seal the lid. Cook the chicken on High Pressure for 17 minutes. Make a quick pressure release. Make the sauce: Mix up double cream, lemon juice, and tahini paste. Slice the chicken and sprinkle it with sauce.

Tangy Meatballs

**Prep time: 10 minutes | Cook time: 10 minutes |
Makes 20 meatballs**

450 g minced chicken
1 egg, lightly beaten
½ medium onion, diced
1 teaspoon garlic powder
1 teaspoon pepper
1 teaspoon salt

240 ml water
Sauce:
2 teaspoons sweetener
1 teaspoon rice vinegar
½ teaspoon sriracha

Stir together the minced chicken, beaten egg, onion, garlic powder, salt, and pepper in a large bowl. Shape into bite-sized balls with your hands. Pour the water into Ninja Foodi Multi-cooker and insert a steamer basket. Put the meatballs in the basket. Secure the lid. Set the cooking time for 10 minutes at High Pressure. Meanwhile, whisk together all ingredients for the sauce in a separate bowl. Once cooking is complete, do a quick pressure release. Carefully open the lid. Toss the meatballs in the prepared sauce and serve.

Chicken Casserole

Prep time: 15 minutes | Cook time: 15 minutes | Serves 4

240 ml broccoli florets
600 ml Alfredo sauce
120 ml chopped fresh spinach
60 ml whole-milk ricotta cheese
½ teaspoon salt

¼ teaspoon pepper
450 g thin-sliced deli chicken
240 ml shredded whole-milk Mozzarella cheese
240 ml water

Put the broccoli florets in a large bowl. Add the Alfredo sauce, spinach, ricotta, salt, and pepper to the bowl and stir to mix well. Using a spoon, separate the veggie mix into three sections. Layer the chicken into the bottom of a 1.8 L glass bowl. Place one section of the veggie mix on top in an even layer and top with a layer of shredded Mozzarella cheese. Repeat until all veggie mix has been used and finish with a layer of Mozzarella cheese. Cover the dish with aluminium foil. Pour the water into the Ninja Foodi Multi-cooker and insert the trivet. Place the dish on the trivet. Secure the lid. Set the cooking time for 15 minutes at High Pressure. Once cooking is complete, do a quick pressure release. Carefully open the lid. If desired, broil in oven for 3 to 5 minutes until golden. Serve warm.

Shredded Buffalo Chicken

Prep time: 10 minutes | Cook time: 20 minutes | Serves 8

2 tablespoons avocado oil
120 ml finely chopped onion
1 celery stalk, finely chopped
1 large carrot, chopped

80 ml mild hot sauce (such as Frank's RedHot)
½ tablespoon apple cider vinegar
¼ teaspoon garlic powder
2 bone-in, skin-on chicken breasts

Set the electric pressure cooker to the Sauté setting. When the pot is hot, pour in the avocado oil. Sauté the onion, celery, and carrot for 3 to 5 minutes or until the onion begins to soften. Hit Start/Stop. Stir in the hot sauce, vinegar, and garlic powder. Place the chicken breasts in the sauce, meat-side down. Close and lock the lid of the pressure cooker. Set the valve to sealing. Cook on high pressure for 20 minutes. When cooking is complete, hit Start/Stop and quick release the pressure. Once the pin drops, unlock and remove the lid. Using tongs, transfer the chicken breasts to a cutting board. When the chicken is cool enough to handle, remove the skin, shred the chicken and return it to the pot. Let the chicken soak in the sauce for at least 5 minutes. Serve immediately.

Peachy Chicken Chunks with Cherries

Prep time: 8 minutes | Cook time: 14 to 16 minutes | Serves 4

100 g peach preserves
1 teaspoon ground rosemary
½ teaspoon black pepper
½ teaspoon salt
½ teaspoon marjoram

1 teaspoon light olive oil
450 g boneless chicken breasts, cut in 1½-inch chunks
Oil for misting or cooking spray
1 (280 g) package frozen unsweetened dark cherries, thawed and drained

In a medium bowl, mix together peach preserves, rosemary, pepper, salt, marjoram, and olive oil. Stir in chicken chunks and toss to coat well with the preserve mixture. Spray the cook & crisp basket with oil or cooking spray and lay chicken chunks in basket. Air crisp at 200°C for 7 minutes. Stir. Cook for 6 to 8 more minutes or until chicken juices run clear. When chicken has cooked through, scatter the cherries over and cook for additional minute to heat cherries.

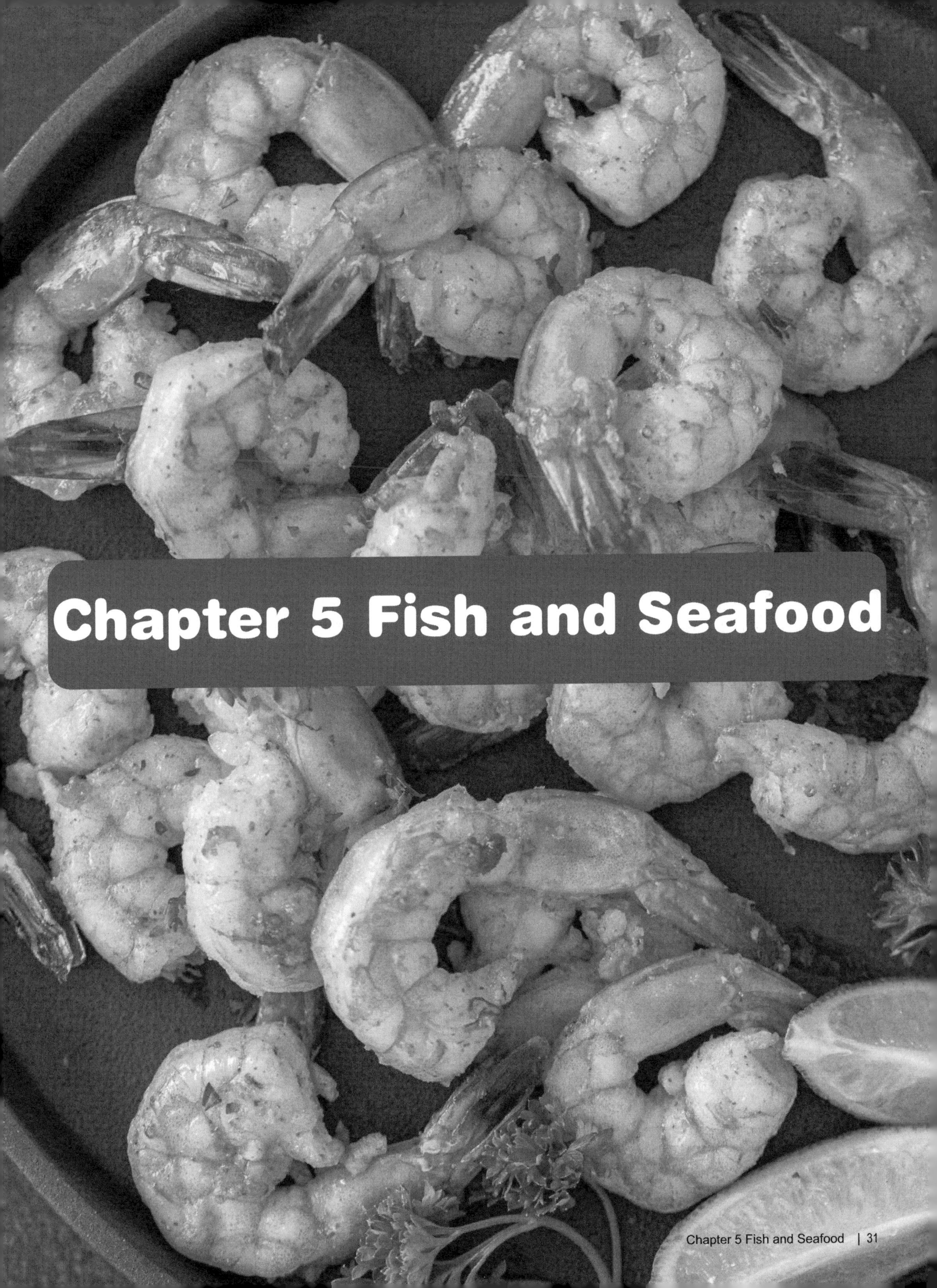

Chapter 5 Fish and Seafood

Chapter 5 Fish and Seafood

Tuna Avocado Bites

Prep time: 10 minutes | Cook time: 7 minutes | Makes 12 bites

280 g can tuna, drained
60 ml full-fat mayonnaise
1 stalk celery, chopped
1 medium avocado, peeled,

pitted, and mashed
50 g blanched finely ground almond flour, divided
2 teaspoons coconut oil

In a large bowl, mix tuna, mayonnaise, celery, and mashed avocado. Form the mixture into balls. Roll balls in almond flour and spritz with coconut oil. Place balls into the cook & crisp basket. Adjust the temperature to 205°C and set the timer for 7 minutes. Gently turn tuna bites after 5 minutes. Serve warm.

Calamari with Hot Sauce

Prep time: 10 minutes | Cook time: 6 minutes | Serves 2

280 g calamari, trimmed
2 tablespoons hot sauce

1 tablespoon avocado oil

Slice the calamari and sprinkle with avocado oil. Put the calamari in the Ninja Foodi Multi-cooker and cook at 205°C for 3 minutes per side. Then transfer the calamari in the serving plate and sprinkle with hot sauce.

Salmon Steaks with Garlicky Yoghurt

Prep time: 2 minutes | Cook time: 4 minutes | Serves 4

240 ml water
2 tablespoons olive oil
4 salmon steaks
Coarse sea salt and ground black pepper, to taste
Garlicky Yoghurt:

1 (230 g) container full-fat Greek yoghurt
2 cloves garlic, minced
2 tablespoons mayonnaise
⅓ teaspoon Dijon mustard

Pour the water into the Ninja Foodi Multi-cooker and insert a trivet. Rub the olive oil into the fish and sprinkle with the salt and black pepper on all sides. Put the fish on the trivet. Lock the lid. Set the cooking time for 4 minutes at High Pressure. When the timer beeps, perform a quick pressure release. Carefully remove the lid. Meanwhile, stir together all the ingredients for the garlicky yoghurt in a bowl. Serve the salmon steaks alongside the garlicky yoghurt.

Scallops and Spinach with Cream Sauce

Prep time: 5 minutes | Cook time: 10 minutes | Serves 2

Vegetable oil spray
280 g frozen spinach, thawed and drained
8 jumbo sea scallops
Kosher or coarse sea salt, and black pepper, to taste

180 ml heavy cream
1 tablespoon tomato paste
1 tablespoon chopped fresh basil
1 teaspoon minced garlic

Spray a baking pan with vegetable oil spray. Spread the thawed spinach in an even layer in the bottom of the pan. Spray both sides of the scallops with vegetable oil spray. Season lightly with salt and pepper. Arrange the scallops on top of the spinach. In a small bowl, whisk together the cream, tomato paste, basil, garlic, ½ teaspoon salt, and ½ teaspoon pepper. Pour the sauce over the scallops and spinach. Place the pan in the cook & crisp basket. Set the Ninja Foodi Multi-cooker to 175°C for 10 minutes. Use a meat thermometer to ensure the scallops have an internal temperature of 55°C.

Greek Prawn with Tomatoes and Feta

Prep time: 10 minutes | Cook time: 2 minutes | Serves 6

3 tablespoons unsalted butter
1 tablespoon garlic
½ teaspoon red pepper flakes, or more as needed
600 ml chopped onion
1 (410 g) can diced tomatoes, undrained

1 teaspoon dried oregano
1 teaspoon salt
450 g frozen prawn, peeled
240 ml crumbled feta cheese
120 ml sliced black olives
60 ml chopped parsley

Preheat the Ninja Foodi Multi-cooker by selecting Sauté and adjusting to high heat. When the inner cooking pot is hot, add the butter and heat until it foams. Add the garlic and red pepper flakes, and cook just until fragrant, about 1 minute. Add the onion, tomatoes, oregano, and salt, and stir to combine. Add the frozen prawn. Lock the lid into place. Adjust the pressure to Low. Cook for 1 minute. When the cooking is complete, quick-release the pressure. Unlock the lid. Mix the prawn in with the lovely tomato broth. Allow the mixture to cool slightly. Right before serving, sprinkle with the feta cheese, olives, and parsley. This dish makes a soupy broth, so it's great over mashed cauliflower.

Pesto Prawns with Wild Rice Pilaf

Prep time: 5 minutes | Cook time: 5 minutes | Serves 4

455 g medium prawns, peeled and deveined

60 g pesto sauce

1 lemon, sliced

390 g cooked wild rice pilaf

Preheat the Ninja Foodi Multi-cooker to 180°C. In a medium bowl, toss the prawns with the pesto sauce until well coated. Place the prawns in a single layer in the cook & crisp basket. Put the lemon slices over the prawns and roast for 5 minutes. Remove the lemons and discard. Serve a quarter of the prawns over 100 g wild rice with some favorite steamed vegetables.

Mussels with Fennel and Leeks

Prep time: 20 minutes | Cook time: 6 minutes | Serves 4

1 tablespoon extra-virgin olive oil, plus extra for drizzling

1 fennel bulb, 1 tablespoon fronds minced, stalks discarded, bulb halved, cored, and sliced thin

1 leek, ends trimmed, leek halved lengthwise, sliced 1 inch

thick, and washed thoroughly

4 garlic cloves, minced

3 sprigs fresh thyme

¼ teaspoon red pepper flakes

120 ml dry white wine

1.4 kg mussels, scrubbed and debearded

Using highest sauté function, heat oil in Ninja Foodi Multi-cooker until shimmering. Add fennel and leek and cook until softened, about 5 minutes. Stir in garlic, thyme sprigs, and pepper flakes and cook until fragrant, about 30 seconds. Stir in wine, then add mussels. Lock lid in place and close pressure release valve. Select high pressure cook function and set cook time for 0 minutes. Once Ninja Foodi Multi-cooker has reached pressure, immediately turn off pot and quick-release pressure. Carefully remove lid, allowing steam to escape away from you. Discard thyme sprigs and any mussels that have not opened. Transfer mussels to individual serving bowls, sprinkle with fennel fronds, and drizzle with extra oil. Serve.

Crispy Fish Nuggets

Prep time: 15 minutes | Cook time: 9 minutes | Serves 4

450 g tilapia fillet

120 ml almond flour

3 eggs, beaten

60 ml avocado oil

1 teaspoon salt

Cut the fish into the small pieces (nuggets) and sprinkle withs alt. Then dip the fish nuggets in the eggs and coat in the almond flour. Heat up avocado oil for 3 minutes on Sauté mode. Put the prepared fish nuggets in the hot oil and cook them on Sauté mode for 3 minutes from each side or until they are golden brown.

Tuna Spinach Cakes

Prep time: 15 minutes | Cook time: 8 minutes | Serves 4

280 g tuna, shredded

240 ml spinach

1 egg, beaten

1 teaspoon ground coriander

2 tablespoon coconut flakes

1 tablespoon avocado oil

Blend the spinach in the blender until smooth. Then transfer it in the mixing bowl and add tuna, egg, and ground coriander. Add coconut flakes and stir the mass with the help of the spoon. Heat up avocado oil in the Ninja Foodi Multi-cooker on Sauté mode for 2 minutes. Then make the medium size cakes from the tuna mixture and place them in the hot oil. Cook the tuna cakes on Sauté mode for 3 minutes. Then flip the on another side and cook for 3 minutes more or until they are light brown.

Tuna Stuffed Poblano Peppers

Prep time: 15 minutes | Cook time: 12 minutes | Serves 4

200 g canned tuna, shredded

1 teaspoon cream cheese

¼ teaspoon minced garlic

60 g Provolone cheese, grated

4 poblano pepper

240 ml water, for cooking

Remove the seeds from poblano peppers. In the mixing bowl, mix up shredded tuna, cream cheese, minced garlic, and grated cheese. Then fill the peppers with tuna mixture and put it in the baking pan. Pour water and insert the baking pan in the Ninja Foodi Multi-cooker. Cook the meal on High Pressure for 12 minutes. Then make a quick pressure release.

Herbed Prawns Pita

Prep time: 5 minutes | Cook time: 8 minutes | Serves 4

455 g medium prawns, peeled and deveined

2 tablespoons olive oil

1 teaspoon dried oregano

½ teaspoon dried thyme

½ teaspoon garlic powder

¼ teaspoon onion powder

½ teaspoon salt

¼ teaspoon black pepper

4 whole wheat pitas

110 g feta cheese, crumbled

75 g shredded lettuce

1 tomato, diced

45 g black olives, sliced

1 lemon

Preheat the oven to 190°C. In a medium bowl, combine the prawns with the olive oil, oregano, thyme, garlic powder, onion powder, salt, and black pepper. Pour prawns in a single layer in the cook & crisp basket and roast for 6 to 8 minutes, or until cooked through. Remove from the Ninja Foodi Multi-cooker and divide into warmed pitas with feta, lettuce, tomato, olives, and a squeeze of lemon.

Cod with Warm Beetroot and Rocket Salad

Prep time: 15 minutes | Cook time: 8 minutes | Serves 4

60 ml extra-virgin olive oil, divided, plus extra for drizzling	broth
1 shallot, sliced thin	1 tablespoon dukkah, plus extra for sprinkling
2 garlic cloves, minced	¼ teaspoon table salt
680 g small beetroots, scrubbed, trimmed, and cut into ½-inch wedges	4 (170 g) skinless cod fillets, 1½ inches thick
120 ml chicken or vegetable	1 tablespoon lemon juice
	60 g baby rocket

Using highest sauté function, heat 1 tablespoon oil in Ninja Foodi Multi-cooker until shimmering. Add shallot and cook until softened, about 2 minutes. Stir in garlic and cook until fragrant, about 30 seconds. Stir in beetroots and broth. Lock lid in place and close pressure release valve. Select high pressure cook function and cook for 3 minutes. Turn off Ninja Foodi Multi-cooker and quick-release pressure. Carefully remove lid, allowing steam to escape away from you. Fold sheet of aluminium foil into 16 by 6-inch sling. Combine 2 tablespoons oil, dukkah, and salt in bowl, then brush cod with oil mixture. Arrange cod skinned side down in center of sling. Using sling, lower cod into Ninja Foodi Multi-cooker; allow narrow edges of sling to rest along sides of insert. Lock lid in place and close pressure release valve. Select high pressure cook function and cook for 2 minutes. Turn off Ninja Foodi Multi-cooker and quick-release pressure. Carefully remove lid, allowing steam to escape away from you. Using sling, transfer cod to large plate. Tent with foil and let rest while finishing beetroot salad. Combine lemon juice and remaining 1 tablespoon oil in large bowl. Using slotted spoon, transfer beetroots to bowl with oil mixture. Add rocket and gently toss to combine. Season with salt and pepper to taste. 5 Serve cod with salad, sprinkling individual portions with extra dukkah and drizzling with extra oil.

Fish Packets with Pesto and Cheese

Prep time: 8 minutes | Cook time: 6 minutes | Serves 4

600 ml cold water.	1 (110 g) jar pesto
4 white fish fillets, such as cod or haddock, 110 g each	120 ml shredded Parmesan cheese (about 60 g)
1 teaspoon fine sea salt	Halved cherry tomatoes, for garnish
½ teaspoon ground black pepper	

Pour the water into your Ninja Foodi Multi-cooker and insert a steamer basket. Sprinkle the fish on all sides with the salt and pepper. Take four sheets of baking paper and place a fillet in the center of each sheet. Dollop 2 tablespoons of the pesto on top of each fillet and sprinkle with 2 tablespoons of the Parmesan cheese. Wrap the fish in the parchment by folding in the edges and folding down the top like an envelope to close tightly. Stack the packets in the steamer basket, seam-side down. Lock the lid. Set the cooking time for 6 minutes at Low Pressure. Once cooking is complete, do a natural pressure release for 10 minutes, then release any remaining pressure. Carefully open the lid. Remove the fish packets from the pot. Transfer to a serving plate and garnish with the cherry tomatoes. Serve immediately.

Lime Lobster Tails

Prep time: 10 minutes | Cook time: 6 minutes | Serves 4

4 lobster tails, peeled	½ teaspoon dried basil
2 tablespoons lime juice	½ teaspoon coconut oil, melted

Mix lobster tails with lime juice, dried basil, and coconut oil. Put the lobster tails in the Ninja Foodi Multi-cooker and cook at 190ºC for 6 minutes.

Honey-Balsamic Salmon

Prep time: 5 minutes | Cook time: 8 minutes | Serves 2

Olive or vegetable oil, for spraying	2 teaspoons red pepper flakes
2 (170 g) salmon fillets	2 teaspoons olive oil
60 ml balsamic vinegar	½ teaspoon salt
2 tablespoons honey	¼ teaspoon freshly ground black pepper

Line the cook & crisp basket with baking paper and spray lightly with oil. Place the salmon in the prepared basket. In a small bowl, whisk together the balsamic vinegar, honey, red pepper flakes, olive oil, salt, and black pepper. Brush the mixture over the salmon. Roast at 200ºC for 7 to 8 minutes, or until the internal temperature reaches 65ºC. Serve immediately.

Flounder Meuniere

Prep time: 15 minutes | Cook time: 10 minutes | Serves 4

450 g flounder fillet	2 tablespoons olive oil
½ teaspoon ground black pepper	1 tablespoon lemon juice
½ teaspoon salt	1 teaspoon chopped fresh parsley
120 ml almond flour	

Cut the fish fillets into 4 servings and sprinkle with salt, ground black pepper, and lemon juice. Heat up the Ninja Foodi Multi-cooker on Sauté mode for 2 minutes and add olive oil. Coat the flounder fillets in the almond flour and put them in the hot olive oil. Sauté the fish fillets for 4 minutes and then flip on another side. Cook the meal for 3 minutes more or until it is golden brown. Sprinkle the cooked flounder with the fresh parsley.

Cajun Salmon

Prep time: 5 minutes | Cook time: 7 minutes | Serves 2

2 salmon fillets, skin removed, 100 g each	pepper
2 tablespoons unsalted butter, melted	½ teaspoon garlic powder
⅛ teaspoon ground cayenne	1 teaspoon paprika
	¼ teaspoon ground black pepper

Brush each fillet with butter. Combine remaining ingredients in a small bowl and then rub onto fish. Place fillets into the cook & crisp basket. Adjust the temperature to 200ºC and air crisp for 7 minutes. When fully cooked, internal temperature will be 65ºC. Serve immediately.

Steamed Cod with Garlic and Swiss Chard

Prep time: 5 minutes | Cook time: 12 minutes | Serves 4

1 teaspoon salt	½ white onion, thinly sliced
½ teaspoon dried oregano	135 g Swiss chard, washed, stemmed, and torn into pieces
½ teaspoon dried thyme	60 ml olive oil
½ teaspoon garlic powder	1 lemon, quartered
4 cod fillets	

Preheat the Ninja Foodi Multi-cooker to 190ºC. In a small bowl, whisk together the salt, oregano, thyme, and garlic powder. Tear off four pieces of aluminum foil, with each sheet being large enough to envelop one cod fillet and a quarter of the vegetables. Place a cod fillet in the middle of each sheet of foil, then sprinkle on all sides with the spice mixture. In each foil packet, place a quarter of the onion slices and 30 g Swiss chard, then drizzle 1 tablespoon olive oil and squeeze ¼ lemon over the contents of each foil packet. Fold and seal the sides of the foil packets and then place them into the cook & crisp basket. Steam for 12 minutes. Remove from the basket, and carefully open each packet to avoid a steam burn.

Lemon-Pepper Trout

Prep time: 5 minutes | Cook time: 15 minutes | Serves 4

4 trout fillets	2 garlic cloves, sliced
2 tablespoons olive oil	1 lemon, sliced, plus additional wedges for serving
½ teaspoon salt	
1 teaspoon black pepper	

Preheat the Ninja Foodi Multi-cooker to 190ºC. Brush each fillet with olive oil on both sides and season with salt and pepper. Place the fillets in an even layer in the cook & crisp basket. Place the sliced garlic over the tops of the trout fillets, then top the garlic with lemon slices and roast for 12 to 15 minutes, or until it has reached an internal temperature of 65ºC. Serve with fresh lemon wedges.

Crab-Stuffed Avocado Boats

Prep time: 5 minutes | Cook time: 7 minutes | Serves 4

2 medium avocados, halved and pitted	2 tablespoons peeled and diced yellow onion
230 g cooked crab meat	2 tablespoons mayonnaise
¼ teaspoon Old Bay seasoning	

Scoop out avocado flesh in each avocado half, leaving ½ inch around edges to form a shell. Chop scooped-out avocado. In a medium bowl, combine crab meat, Old Bay seasoning, onion, mayonnaise, and chopped avocado. Place ¼ mixture into each avocado shell. Place avocado boats into ungreased cook & crisp basket. Adjust the temperature to 175ºC and air crisp for 7 minutes. Avocado will be browned on the top and mixture will be bubbling when done. Serve warm.

Tuna-Stuffed Tomatoes

Prep time: 5 minutes | Cook time: 5 minutes | Serves 2

2 medium beefsteak tomatoes, tops removed, seeded, membranes removed	2 tablespoons mayonnaise
2 (75 g) g tuna fillets packed in water, drained	¼ teaspoon salt
1 medium stalk celery, trimmed and chopped	¼ teaspoon ground black pepper
	2 teaspoons coconut oil
	25 g shredded mild Cheddar cheese

Scoop pulp out of each tomato, leaving ½-inch shell. In a medium bowl, mix tuna, celery, mayonnaise, salt, and pepper. Drizzle with coconut oil. Spoon ½ mixture into each tomato and top each with 2 tablespoons Cheddar. Place tomatoes into ungreased cook & crisp basket. Adjust the temperature to 160ºC and air crisp for 5 minutes. Cheese will be melted when done. Serve warm.

Mediterranean-Style Cod

Prep time: 5 minutes | Cook time: 12 minutes | Serves 4

4 cod fillets, 170 g each	6 cherry tomatoes, halved
3 tablespoons fresh lemon juice	45 g pitted and sliced kalamata olives
1 tablespoon olive oil	
¼ teaspoon salt	

Place cod into an ungreased round nonstick baking dish. Pour lemon juice into dish and drizzle cod with olive oil. Sprinkle with salt. Place tomatoes and olives around baking dish in between fillets. Place dish into cook & crisp basket. Adjust the temperature to 175ºC and bake for 12 minutes, carefully turning cod halfway through cooking. Fillets will be lightly browned, easily flake, and have an internal temperature of at least 65ºC when done. Serve warm.

Dill Lemon Salmon

Prep time: 10 minutes | Cook time: 4 minutes | Serves 4

450 g salmon fillet
1 tablespoon butter, melted
2 tablespoons lemon juice
1 teaspoon dried dill
240 ml water

Cut the salmon fillet on 4 servings. Line the Ninja Foodi Multi-cooker baking pan with foil and put the salmon fillets inside in one layer. Then sprinkle the fish with dried dill, lemon juice, and butter. Pour water in the Ninja Foodi Multi-cooker and insert the rack. Place the baking pan with salmon on the rack and close the lid. Cook the meal on High Pressure for 4 minutes. Allow the natural pressure release for 5 minutes and remove the fish from the Ninja Foodi Multi-cooker.

Lemony Prawns

Prep time: 10 minutes | Cook time: 7 to 8 minutes | Serves 4

455 g prawns, peeled and deveined
4 tablespoons olive oil
1½ tablespoons lemon juice
1½ tablespoons fresh parsley, roughly chopped
2 cloves garlic, finely minced
1 teaspoon crushed red pepper flakes, or more to taste
Garlic pepper, to taste
Sea salt flakes, to taste

Preheat the Ninja Foodi Multi-cooker to 195°C. Toss all the ingredients in a large bowl until the prawns are coated on all sides. Arrange the prawns in the cook & crisp basket and air crisp for 7 to 8 minutes, or until the prawns are pink and cooked through. Serve warm.

Cilantro Lime Baked Salmon

Prep time: 10 minutes | Cook time: 12 minutes | Serves 2

2 salmon fillets, 85 g each, skin removed
1 tablespoon salted butter, melted
1 teaspoon chilli powder
½ teaspoon finely minced garlic
20 g sliced pickled jalapeños
½ medium lime, juiced
2 tablespoons chopped coriander

Place salmon fillets into a round baking pan. Brush each with butter and sprinkle with chilli powder and garlic. Place jalapeño slices on top and around salmon. Pour half of the lime juice over the salmon and cover with foil. Place pan into the cook & crisp basket. Adjust the temperature to 190°C and bake for 12 minutes. When fully cooked, salmon should flake easily with a fork and reach an internal temperature of at least 65°C. To serve, spritz with remaining lime juice and garnish with coriander.

Steamed Halibut with Lemon

Prep time: 10 minutes | Cook time: 9 minutes | Serves 3

3 halibut fillet
½ lemon, sliced
½ teaspoon white pepper
½ teaspoon ground coriander
1 tablespoon avocado oil
240 ml water, for cooking

Pour water and insert the steamer rack in the Ninja Foodi Multi-cooker. Rub the fish fillets with white pepper, ground coriander, and avocado oil. Place the fillets in the steamer rack. Then top the halibut with sliced lemon. Close and seal the lid. Cook the meal on High Pressure for 9 minutes. Make a quick pressure release.

Black Cod with Grapes and Kale

Prep time: 10 minutes | Cook time: 15 minutes | Serves 2

2 fillets of black cod, 200 g each
Salt and freshly ground black pepper, to taste
Olive oil
150 g grapes, halved
1 small bulb fennel, sliced
¼-inch thick
65 g pecans
200 g shredded kale
2 teaspoons white balsamic vinegar or white wine vinegar
2 tablespoons extra-virgin olive oil

Preheat the Ninja Foodi Multi-cooker to 205°C. Season the cod fillets with salt and pepper and drizzle, brush or spray a little olive oil on top. Place the fish, presentation side up (skin side down), into the cook & crisp basket. Air crisp for 10 minutes. When the fish has finished cooking, remove the fillets to a side plate and loosely tent with foil to rest. Toss the grapes, fennel and pecans in a bowl with a drizzle of olive oil and season with salt and pepper. Add the grapes, fennel and pecans to the cook & crisp basket and air crisp for 5 minutes, shaking the basket once during the cooking time. Transfer the grapes, fennel and pecans to a bowl with the kale. Dress the kale with the balsamic vinegar and olive oil, season to taste with salt and pepper and serve alongside the cooked fish.

Louisiana Prawn Gumbo

Prep time: 10 minutes | Cook time: 4 minutes | Serves 6

450 g prawn
60 ml chopped celery stalk
1 chili pepper, chopped
60 ml chopped okra
1 tablespoon coconut oil
480 ml chicken broth
1 teaspoon sugar-free tomato paste

Put all ingredients in the Ninja Foodi Multi-cooker and stir until you get a light red colour. Then close and seal the lid. Cook the meal on High Pressure for 4 minutes. When the time is finished, allow the natural pressure release for 10 minutes.

Italian Salmon

Prep time: 10 minutes | Cook time: 4 minutes | Serves 2

280 g salmon fillet
1 teaspoon Italian seasoning

240 ml water

Pour water and insert the trivet in the Ninja Foodi Multi-cooker. Then rub the salmon fillet with Italian seasoning and wrap in the foil. Place the wrapped fish on the trivet and close the lid. Cook the meal on High Pressure for 4 minutes. Make a quick pressure release and remove the fish from the foil. Cut it into servings.

Butter-Wine Baked Salmon

Prep time: 5 minutes | Cook time: 10 minutes | Serves 4

4 tablespoons butter, melted
2 cloves garlic, minced
Sea salt and ground black pepper, to taste
60 ml dry white wine or apple cider vinegar

1 tablespoon lime juice
1 teaspoon smoked paprika
½ teaspoon onion powder
4 salmon steaks
Cooking spray

Place all the ingredients except the salmon and oil in a shallow dish and stir to mix well. Add the salmon steaks, turning to coat well on both sides. Transfer the salmon to the refrigerator to marinate for 30 minutes. Preheat the Ninja Foodi Multi-cooker to 180°C. Place the salmon steaks in the cook & crisp basket, discarding any excess marinade. Spray the salmon steaks with cooking spray. Air crisp for about 10 minutes, flipping the salmon steaks halfway through, or until cooked to your preferred doneness. Divide the salmon steaks among four plates and serve.

Lemon Butter Mahi Mahi

Prep time: 10 minutes | Cook time: 9 minutes | Serves 4

450 g mahi-mahi fillet
1 teaspoon grated lemon zest
1 tablespoon lemon juice

1 tablespoon butter, softened
½ teaspoon salt
240 ml water, for cooking

Cut the fish on 4 servings and sprinkle with lemon zest, lemon juice, salt, and rub with softened butter. Then put the fish in the baking pan in one layer. Pour water and insert the steamer rack in the Ninja Foodi Multi-cooker. Put the mold with fish on the rack. Close and seal the lid. Cook the Mahi Mahi on High Pressure for 9 minutes. Make a quick pressure release.

One-Pot Prawn Fried Rice

Prep time: 10 minutes | Cook time: 25 minutes | Serves 4

Prawns:
1 teaspoon cornflour
½ teaspoon kosher or coarse sea salt
¼ teaspoon black pepper
455 g jumbo raw prawns (21 to 25 count), peeled and deveined
Rice:
200 g cold cooked rice
140 g frozen peas and carrots, thawed
235 g chopped spring onions

(white and green parts)
3 tablespoons toasted sesame oil
1 tablespoon soy sauce
½ teaspoon kosher or coarse sea salt
1 teaspoon black pepper
Eggs:
2 large eggs, beaten
¼ teaspoon kosher or coarse sea salt
¼ teaspoon black pepper

For the prawns: In a small bowl, whisk together the cornflour, salt, and pepper until well combined. Place the prawns in a large bowl and sprinkle the seasoned cornflour over. Toss until well coated; set aside. For the rice: In a baking pan, combine the rice, peas and carrots, spring onions, sesame oil, soy sauce, salt, and pepper. Toss and stir until well combined. Place the pan in the cook & crisp basket. Set the Ninja Foodi Multi-cooker to 175°C for 15 minutes, stirring and tossing the rice halfway through the cooking time. Place the prawns on top of the rice. Cook for 5 minutes. Meanwhile, for the eggs: In a medium bowl, beat the eggs with the salt and pepper. Open the Ninja Foodi Multi-cooker and pour the eggs over the prawns and rice mixture. Cook for 5 minutes. Remove the pan from the Ninja Foodi Multi-cooker. Stir to break up the rice and mix in the eggs and prawns.

Chapter 6 Beef, Pork, and Lamb

Chapter 6 Beef, Pork, and Lamb

Southern Chili

Prep time: 20 minutes | Cook time: 25 minutes | Serves 4

450 g beef mince (85% lean)
235 ml minced onion
1 (794 g) can tomato purée
1 (425 g) can diced tomatoes

1 (425 g) can red kidney beans, rinsed and drained
60 ml Chili seasoning

Preheat the Ninja Foodi Multi-cooker to 205°C. In a baking pan, mix the mince and onion. Place the pan in the Ninja Foodi Multi-cooker. Cook for 4 minutes. Stir and cook for 4 minutes more until browned. Remove the pan from the fryer. Drain the meat and transfer to a large bowl. Reduce the Ninja Foodi Multi-cooker temperature to 175°C. To the bowl with the meat, add in the tomato purée, diced tomatoes, kidney beans, and Chili seasoning. Mix well. Pour the mixture into the baking pan. Cook for 25 minutes, stirring every 10 minutes, until thickened.

Pork Milanese

Prep time: 10 minutes | Cook time: 12 minutes | Serves 4

4 (1-inch) boneless pork chops
Fine sea salt and ground black pepper, to taste
2 large eggs
180 ml pre-grated Parmesan

cheese
Chopped fresh parsley, for garnish
Lemon slices, for serving

Spray the cook & crisp basket with avocado oil. Preheat the Ninja Foodi Multi-cooker to 205°C. Place the pork chops between 2 sheets of plastic wrap and pound them with the flat side of a meat tenderizer until they're ¼ inch thick. Lightly season both sides of the chops with salt and pepper. Lightly beat the eggs in a shallow bowl. Divide the Parmesan cheese evenly between 2 bowls and set the bowls in this order: Parmesan, eggs, Parmesan. Dredge a chop in the first bowl of Parmesan, then dip it in the eggs, and then dredge it again in the second bowl of Parmesan, making sure both sides and all edges are well coated. Repeat with the remaining chops. Place the chops in the cook & crisp basket and air crisp for 12 minutes, or until the internal temperature reaches 65°C, flipping halfway through. Garnish with fresh parsley and serve immediately with lemon slices. Store leftovers in an airtight container in the refrigerator for up to 3 days. Reheat in a preheated 200°C Ninja Foodi Multi-cooker for 5 minutes, or until warmed through.

Smoky Pork Tenderloin

Prep time: 5 minutes | Cook time: 19 to 22 minutes | Serves 6

680 g pork tenderloin
1 tablespoon avocado oil
1 teaspoon chili powder
1 teaspoon smoked paprika

1 teaspoon garlic powder
1 teaspoon sea salt
1 teaspoon freshly ground black pepper

Pierce the tenderloin all over with a fork and rub the oil all over the meat. In a small dish, stir together the chili powder, smoked paprika, garlic powder, salt, and pepper. Rub the spice mixture all over the tenderloin. Set the Ninja Foodi Multi-cooker to 205°C. Place the pork in the cook & crisp basket and air crisp for 10 minutes. Flip the tenderloin and cook for 9 to 12 minutes more, until an instant-read thermometer reads at least 65°C. Allow the tenderloin to rest for 5 minutes, then slice and serve.

Pork Taco Casserole

Prep time: 15 minutes | Cook time: 30 minutes | Serves 6

120 ml water
2 eggs
85 g Cottage cheese, at room temperature
60 ml double cream
1 teaspoon taco seasoning
170 g Cotija cheese, crumbled

340 g minced pork
120 ml tomatoes, puréed
1 tablespoon taco seasoning
85 g chopped green chilies
170 g Queso Manchego cheese, shredded

Add the water in the Ninja Foodi Multi-cooker and place in the trivet. In a mixing bowl, combine the eggs, Cottage cheese, double cream, and taco seasoning. Lightly grease a casserole dish. Spread the Cotija cheese over the bottom. Stir in the egg mixture. Lower the casserole dish onto the trivet. Secure the lid. Set cooking time for 20 minutes on High Pressure. Once cooking is complete, use a quick pressure release. Carefully remove the lid. In the meantime, heat a skillet over a medium-high heat. Brown the minced pork, crumbling with a fork. Add the tomato purée, taco seasoning, and green chilies. Spread the mixture over the prepared cheese crust. Top with shredded Queso Manchego. Secure the lid. Set cooking time for 10 minutes on High Pressure. Once cooking is complete, use a quick pressure release. Carefully remove the lid. Serve immediately.

Bone Broth Brisket with Tomatoes

Prep time: 5 minutes | Cook time: 75 minutes | Serves 4 to 5

2 tablespoons coconut oil	black pepper
½ teaspoon garlic salt	1 (400 g) can sugar-free or low-sugar diced tomatoes
½ teaspoon crushed red pepper	
½ teaspoon dried basil	240 ml grass-fed bone broth
½ teaspoon rock salt	450 g beef brisket, chopped
½ teaspoon freshly ground	

Set the Ninja Foodi Multi-cooker to Sauté and melt the oil. Mix the garlic salt, red pepper, basil, rock salt, black pepper, and tomatoes in a medium bowl. Pour bone broth into the Ninja Foodi Multi-cooker, then add the brisket, and top with the premixed sauce. Close the lid, set the pressure release to Sealing, and hit Start/Stop to stop the current program. Set the Ninja Foodi Multi-cooker to 75 minutes on High Pressure, and let cook. Once cooked, carefully switch the pressure release to Venting. Open the Ninja Foodi Multi-cooker, and serve. You can pour remaining sauce over brisket, if desired.

Spicy Bavette Steak with Zhoug

Prep time: 30 minutes | Cook time: 8 minutes | Serves 4

Marinade and Steak:	680 g bavette or skirt steak, trimmed and cut into 3 pieces
120 ml dark beer or orange juice	
60 ml fresh lemon juice	Zhoug:
3 cloves garlic, minced	235 ml packed fresh coriander leaves
2 tablespoons extra-virgin olive oil	2 cloves garlic, peeled
2 tablespoons Sriracha	2 jalapeño or green chiles, stemmed and coarsely chopped
2 tablespoons brown sugar	½ teaspoon ground cumin
2 teaspoons ground cumin	¼ teaspoon ground coriander
2 teaspoons smoked paprika	¼ teaspoon coarse or flaky salt
1 tablespoon coarse or flaky salt	2 to 4 tablespoons extra-virgin olive oil
1 teaspoon black pepper	

For the marinade and steak: In a small bowl, whisk together the beer, lemon juice, garlic, olive oil, Sriracha, brown sugar, cumin, paprika, salt, and pepper. Place the steak in a large resealable plastic bag. Pour the marinade over the steak, seal the bag, and massage the steak to coat. Marinate in the refrigerator for 1 hour or up to 24 hours, turning the bag occasionally. Meanwhile, for the zhoug: In a food processor, combine the coriander, garlic, jalapeños, cumin, coriander, and salt. Process until finely chopped. Add 2 tablespoons olive oil and pulse to form a loose paste, adding up to 2 tablespoons more olive oil if needed. Transfer the zhoug to a glass container. Cover and store in the refrigerator until 30 minutes before serving if marinating more than 1 hour. Remove the steak from the marinade and discard the marinade. Place the steak in the cook & crisp basket and set the Ninja Foodi Multi-cooker to 205ºC for 8 minutes. Use a meat thermometer to ensure the steak has reached an internal temperature of 65ºC (for medium). Transfer the steak to a cutting board and let rest for 5 minutes. Slice the steak across the grain and serve with the zhoug.

Sumptuous Pizza Tortilla Rolls

Prep time: 10 minutes | Cook time: 6 minutes | Serves 4

1 teaspoon butter	8 flour tortillas
½ medium onion, slivered	8 thin slices wafer-thinham
½ red or green pepper, julienned	24 pepperoni slices
110 g fresh white mushrooms, chopped	235 ml shredded Mozzarella cheese
120 ml pizza sauce	Cooking spray

Preheat the Ninja Foodi Multi-cooker to 200ºC. Put butter, onions, pepper, and mushrooms in a baking pan. Bake in the preheated Ninja Foodi Multi-cooker for 3 minutes. Stir and cook 3 to 4 minutes longer until just crisp and tender. Remove pan and set aside. To assemble rolls, spread about 2 teaspoons of pizza sauce on one half of each tortilla. Top with a slice of ham and 3 slices of pepperoni. Divide sautéed vegetables among tortillas and top with cheese. Roll up tortillas, secure with toothpicks if needed, and spray with oil. Put 4 rolls in cook & crisp basket and air crisp for 4 minutes. Turn and air crisp 4 minutes, until heated through and lightly browned. Repeat step 4 to air crisp remaining pizza rolls. Serve immediately.

Beery Boston-Style Butt

Prep time: 10 minutes | Cook time: 1 hour 1 minutes | Serves 4

1 tablespoon butter	Pinch of grated nutmeg
450 g Boston-style butt	Sea salt, to taste
120 ml leeks, chopped	¼ teaspoon ground black pepper
60 ml beer	
120 ml chicken stock	60 ml water

Press the Sauté button to heat up the Ninja Foodi Multi-cooker. Once hot, melt the butter. Cook the Boston-style butt for 3 minutes on each side. Remove from the pot and reserve. Sauté the leeks for 5 minutes or until fragrant. Add the remaining ingredients and stir to combine. Secure the lid. Set cooking time for 50 minutes on High pressure. Once cooking is complete, use a natural pressure release for 20 minutes, then release any remaining pressure. Carefully remove the lid. Serve immediately.

Greek Lamb Pitta Pockets

Prep time: 15 minutes | Cook time: 6 minutes | Serves 4

Dressing:
235 ml plain yogurt
1 tablespoon lemon juice
1 teaspoon dried dill, crushed
1 teaspoon ground oregano
½ teaspoon salt
Meatballs:
230 g lamb mince
1 tablespoon diced onion
1 teaspoon dried parsley
1 teaspoon dried dill, crushed
¼ teaspoon oregano

¼ teaspoon coriander
¼ teaspoon ground cumin
¼ teaspoon salt
4 pitta halves
Suggested Toppings:
1 red onion, slivered
1 medium cucumber, deseeded, thinly sliced
Crumbled feta cheese
Sliced black olives
Chopped fresh peppers

Preheat the Ninja Foodi Multi-cooker to 200ºC. Stir the dressing ingredients together in a small bowl and refrigerate while preparing lamb. Combine all meatball ingredients in a large bowl and stir to distribute seasonings. Shape meat mixture into 12 small meatballs, rounded or slightly flattened if you prefer. Transfer the meatballs in the preheated Ninja Foodi Multi-cooker and air crisp for 6 minutes, until well done. Remove and drain on paper towels. To serve, pile meatballs and the choice of toppings in pitta pockets and drizzle with dressing.

Herbed Pork Roast with Asparagus

Prep time: 25 minutes | Cook time: 17 minutes | Serves 6

1 teaspoon dried thyme
½ teaspoon garlic powder
½ teaspoon onion powder
½ teaspoon dried oregano
1½ teaspoons smoked paprika
½ teaspoon ground black pepper
1 teaspoon sea salt
2 tablespoons olive oil, divided
900 g boneless pork loin roast

½ medium white onion, chopped
2 garlic cloves, minced
160 ml chicken broth
2 tablespoons Worcestershire sauce
240 ml water
20 fresh asparagus spears, cut in half and woody ends removed

In a small bowl, combine the thyme, garlic powder, onion powder, oregano, smoked paprika, black pepper, and sea salt. Mix until well combined and then add 1½ tablespoons olive oil. Stir until blended. Brush all sides of the pork roast with the oil and spice mixture. Place the roast in a covered dish and transfer to the refrigerator to marinate for 30 minutes. Select Sauté mode and brush the Ninja Foodi Multi-cooker with remaining olive oil. Once the oil is hot, add the pork roast and sear for 5 minutes per side or until browned. Remove the roast from the pot and set aside. Add the onions and garlic to the pot and Sauté for 2 minutes, or until the onions soften and garlic becomes fragrant. Add the chicken broth and Worcestershire sauce. Lock the lid. Set cooking time for 15 minutes on High pressure. When cooking is complete, allow the pressure release naturally for 10 minutes and then release the remaining pressure. Open the lid. Transfer the roast to a cutting board, cover with aluminium foil, and set aside to rest. Transfer the broth to a measuring cup. Set aside. Place the trivet in the Ninja Foodi Multi-cooker and add the water to the bottom of the pot. Place the asparagus in an ovenproof bowl that will fit in the Ninja Foodi Multi-cooker and place the bowl on top of the trivet. Lock the lid. Select Steam mode and set cooking time for 2 minutes. Once the cook time is complete, quick release the pressure. Open the lid and transfer the asparagus to a large serving platter. Thinly slice the roast and transfer to the serving platter with the asparagus. Drizzle the reserved broth over top. Serve warm.

Pork Carnitas

Prep time: 10 minutes | Cook time: 20 minutes | Serves 8

1 teaspoon rock salt
2 teaspoons chili powder
2 teaspoons dried oregano
½ teaspoon freshly ground black pepper
1 (1.2 kg) pork sirloin roast or boneless pork butt, cut into 1½-inch cubes
2 tablespoons avocado oil, divided
3 garlic cloves, minced

Juice and zest of 1 large orange
Juice and zest of 1 medium lime
6-inch gluten-free corn tortillas, warmed, for serving (optional)
Chopped avocado, for serving (optional)
Roasted Tomatillo Salsa or salsa verde, for serving (optional)
Shredded cheddar cheese, for serving (optional)

In a large bowl or gallon-size zip-top bag, combine the salt, chili powder, oregano, and pepper. Add the pork cubes and toss to coat. Set the electric pressure cooker to the Sauté setting. When the pot is hot, pour in 1 tablespoon of avocado oil. Add half of the pork to the pot and sear until the pork is browned on all sides, about 5 minutes. Transfer the pork to a plate, add the remaining 1 tablespoon of avocado oil to the pot, and sear the remaining pork. Hit Start/Stop. Return all of the pork to the pot and add the garlic, orange zest and juice, and lime zest and juice to the pot. Close and lock the lid of the pressure cooker. Set the valve to sealing. Cook on high pressure for 20 minutes. When the cooking is complete, hit Start/Stop. Allow the pressure to release naturally for 15 minutes then quick release any remaining pressure. Once the pin drops, unlock and remove the lid. Using two forks, shred the meat right in the pot. (Optional) For more authentic carnitas, spread the shredded meat on a broiler-safe baking tray. Preheat the broiler with the rack 6 inches from the heating element. Broil the pork for about 5 minutes or until it begins to crisp. (Watch carefully so you don't let the pork burn.) Place the pork in a serving bowl. Top with some of the juices from the pot. Serve with tortillas, avocado, salsa, and Cheddar cheese (if using).

Chinese-Style Baby Back Ribs

Prep time: 30 minutes | Cook time: 30 minutes | Serves 4

1 tablespoon toasted sesame oil	1 tablespoon agave nectar or honey
1 tablespoon fermented black bean paste	1 teaspoon minced garlic
1 tablespoon Shaoxing wine (rice cooking wine)	1 teaspoon minced fresh ginger
1 tablespoon dark soy sauce	1 (680 g) slab baby back ribs, cut into individual ribs

In a large bowl, stir together the sesame oil, black bean paste, wine, soy sauce, agave, garlic, and ginger. Add the ribs and toss well to coat. Marinate at room temperature for 30 minutes, or cover and refrigerate for up to 24 hours. Place the ribs in the cook & crisp basket; discard the marinade. Set the Ninja Foodi Multi-cooker to 175ºC for 30 minutes.

Air Fried Crispy Venison

Prep time: 10 minutes | Cook time: 20 minutes | Serves 4

2 eggs	pepper
60 ml milk	450 g venison backstrap/striploin, sliced
235 ml whole wheat flour	Cooking spray
½ teaspoon salt	
¼ teaspoon ground black	

Preheat the Ninja Foodi Multi-cooker to 180ºC and spritz with cooking spray. Whisk the eggs with milk in a large bowl. Combine the flour with salt and ground black pepper in a shallow dish. Dredge the venison in the flour first, then into the egg mixture. Shake the excess off and roll the venison back over the flour to coat well. Arrange half of the venison in the preheated Ninja Foodi Multi-cooker and spritz with cooking spray. Air crisp for 10 minutes or until the internal temperature of the venison reaches at least 65ºC for medium rare. Flip the venison halfway through. Repeat with remaining venison. Serve immediately.

Herb-Roasted Beef Tips with Onions

Prep time: 5 minutes | Cook time: 10 minutes | Serves 4

450 g rib eye steak, cubed	1 teaspoon salt
2 garlic cloves, minced	½ teaspoon black pepper
2 tablespoons olive oil	1 brown onion, thinly sliced
1 tablespoon fresh oregano	

Preheat the Ninja Foodi Multi-cooker to 190ºC. In a medium bowl, combine the steak, garlic, olive oil, oregano, salt, pepper, and onion. Mix until all of the beef and onion are well coated. Put the seasoned steak mixture into the cook & crisp basket. Roast for 5 minutes. Stir and roast for 5 minutes more. Let rest for 5 minutes before serving with some favorite sides.

Beef Burger

Prep time: 20 minutes | Cook time: 12 minutes | Serves 4

570 g lean beef mince	½ teaspoon cumin powder
1 tablespoon soy sauce or tamari	60 ml spring onions, minced
1 teaspoon Dijon mustard	⅓ teaspoon sea salt flakes
1/2 teaspoon smoked paprika	⅓ teaspoon freshly cracked mixed peppercorns
1 teaspoon shallot powder	1 teaspoon celery salt
1 clove garlic, minced	1 teaspoon dried parsley

Mix all of the above ingredients in a bowl; knead until everything is well incorporated. Shape the mixture into four patties. Next, make a shallow dip in the center of each patty to prevent them puffing up during air crisping. Spritz the patties on all sides using nonstick cooking spray. Cook approximately 12 minutes at 180ºC. Check for doneness, an instant-read thermometer should read 70ºC. Bon appétit!

Pork Adobo

Prep time: 10 minutes | Cook time: 30 minutes | Serves 6

450 g pork belly, chopped	vinegar
1 bay leaf	1 teaspoon cayenne pepper
1 teaspoon salt	1 garlic clove, peeled
2 tablespoons apple cider	480 ml water

Put all ingredients in the Ninja Foodi Multi-cooker. Close and seal the lid. Cook Adobo pork for 30 minutes on High Pressure. When the cooking time is finished, make a quick pressure release and transfer the pork belly in the bowls. Add 1 ladle of the pork gravy.

Beef Shami Kabob

Prep time: 15 minutes | Cook time: 35 minutes | Serves 4

450 g beef chunks, chopped	60 ml almond flour
1 teaspoon ginger paste	1 egg, beaten
½ teaspoon ground cumin	1 tablespoon coconut oil
480 ml water	

Put the beef chunks, ginger paste, ground cumin, and water in the Ninja Foodi Multi-cooker. Set cooking time for 30 minutes on High Pressure. When timer beeps, make a quick pressure release. Open the lid. Drain the water from the meat. Transfer the beef in the blender. Add the almond flour and beaten egg. Blend until smooth. Shape the mixture into small meatballs. Heat the coconut oil on Sauté mode and put the meatballs inside. Cook for 2 minutes on each side or until golden brown. Serve immediately.

Ginger Beef Flank Steak

Prep time: 8 minutes | Cook time: 13 minutes | Serves 2

400 g beef flank steak, sliced
1 tablespoon almond flour
½ teaspoon minced ginger
30 g spring onions, sliced
1 tablespoon coconut oil
180 ml water

Toss the beef strips in the almond flour and shake well. Toss the coconut oil in the Ninja Foodi Multi-cooker bowl and set the Sauté mode. When the coconut oil is melted, add the beef flank steak slices and cook them for 3 minutes. Stir them from time to time. Add minced ginger. Pour the water over the meat and lock the Ninja Foodi Multi-cooker lid. Choose High Pressure and set the timer for 10 minutes. Make a quick pressure release. Top the cooked beef with sliced spring onions.

Minute Steak Roll-Ups

Prep time: 30 minutes | Cook time: 8 to 10 minutes | Serves 4

4 minute steaks (170 g each)
1 (450 g) bottle Italian dressing
1 teaspoon salt
½ teaspoon freshly ground black pepper
120 ml finely chopped brown
onion
120 ml finely chopped green pepper
120 ml finely chopped mushrooms
1 to 2 tablespoons oil

In a large resealable bag or airtight storage container, combine the steaks and Italian dressing. Seal the bag and refrigerate to marinate for 2 hours. Remove the steaks from the marinade and place them on a cutting board. Discard the marinade. Evenly season the steaks with salt and pepper. In a small bowl, stir together the onion, pepper, and mushrooms. Sprinkle the onion mixture evenly over the steaks. Roll up the steaks, jelly roll-style, and secure with toothpicks. Preheat the Ninja Foodi Multi-cooker to 205°C. Place the steaks in the cook & crisp basket. Cook for 4 minutes. Flip the steaks and spritz them with oil. Cook for 4 to 6 minutes more until the internal temperature reaches 65°C. Let rest for 5 minutes before serving.

Rosemary Lamb Chops

Prep time: 25 minutes | Cook time: 2 minutes | Serves 4

680 g lamb chops (4 small chops)
1 teaspoon rock salt
Leaves from 1 (6-inch) rosemary sprig
2 tablespoons avocado oil
1 shallot, peeled and cut in quarters
1 tablespoon tomato paste
240 ml beef broth

Place the lamb chops on a cutting board. Press the salt and rosemary leaves into both sides of the chops. Let rest at room temperature for 15 to 30 minutes. Set the electric pressure cooker to Sauté setting. When hot, add the avocado oil. Brown the lamb chops, about 2 minutes per side. (If they don't all fit in a single layer, brown them in batches.) Transfer the chops to a plate. In the pot, combine the shallot, tomato paste, and broth. Cook for about a minute, scraping up the brown bits from the bottom. Hit Start/Stop. Add the chops and any accumulated juices back to the pot. Close and lock the lid of the pressure cooker. Set the valve to sealing. Cook on high pressure for 2 minutes. When the cooking is complete, hit Start/Stop and quick release the pressure. Once the pin drops, unlock and remove the lid. Place the lamb chops on plates and serve immediately.

Ham Hock Mac and Cheese

Prep time: 20 minutes | Cook time: 25 minutes | Serves 4

2 large eggs, beaten
475 ml cottage cheese, full-fat or low-fat
475 ml grated sharp Cheddar cheese, divided
235 ml sour cream
½ teaspoon salt
1 teaspoon freshly ground black pepper
475 ml uncooked elbow macaroni
2 ham hocks (about 310 g each), meat removed and diced
1 to 2 tablespoons oil

In a large bowl, stir together the eggs, cottage cheese, 235 ml of the Cheddar cheese, sour cream, salt, and pepper. Stir in the macaroni and the diced meat. Preheat the Ninja Foodi Multi-cooker to 180°C. Spritz a baking pan with oil. Pour the macaroni mixture into the prepared pan, making sure all noodles are covered with sauce. Cook for 12 minutes. Stir in the remaining 235 ml of Cheddar cheese, making sure all the noodles are covered with sauce. Cook for 13 minutes more, until the noodles are tender. Let rest for 5 minutes before serving.

Kale and Beef Omelet

Prep time: 15 minutes | Cook time: 16 minutes | Serves 4

230 g leftover beef, coarsely chopped
2 garlic cloves, pressed
235 ml kale, torn into pieces and wilted
1 tomato, chopped
¼ teaspoon sugar
4 eggs, beaten
4 tablespoons double cream
½ teaspoon turmeric powder
Salt and ground black pepper, to taste
⅛ teaspoon ground allspice
Cooking spray

Preheat the Ninja Foodi Multi-cooker to 180°C. Spritz four ramekins with cooking spray. Put equal amounts of each of the ingredients into each ramekin and mix well. Air crisp for 16 minutes. Serve immediately.

Braised Pork Belly

Prep time: 15 minutes | Cook time: 37 minutes | Serves 4

450 g pork belly
1 tablespoon olive oil
Salt and ground black pepper to taste

1 clove garlic, minced
240 ml dry white wine
Rosemary sprig

Select the Sauté mode on the Ninja Foodi Multi-cooker and heat the oil. Add the pork belly and sauté for 2 minutes per side, until starting to brown. Season the meat with salt and pepper, add the garlic. Pour in the wine and add the rosemary sprig. Bring to a boil. Set the cooking time for 35 minutes at High pressure. Once cooking is complete, use a natural pressure release for 10 minutes, then release any remaining pressure. Open the lid. Slice the meat and serve.

Sausage and Cauliflower Arancini

Prep time: 30 minutes | Cook time: 28 to 32 minutes
| Serves 6

Avocado oil spray
170 g Italian-seasoned sausage, casings removed
60 ml diced onion
1 teaspoon minced garlic
1 teaspoon dried thyme
Sea salt and freshly ground black pepper, to taste
120 ml cauliflower rice

85 g cream cheese
110 g Cheddar cheese, shredded
1 large egg
120 ml finely ground blanched almond flour
60 ml finely grated Parmesan cheese
Keto-friendly marinara sauce, for serving

Spray a large skillet with oil and place it over medium-high heat. Once the skillet is hot, put the sausage in the skillet and cook for 7 minutes, breaking up the meat with the back of a spoon. Reduce the heat to medium and add the onion. Cook for 5 minutes, then add the garlic, thyme, and salt and pepper to taste. Cook for 1 minute more. Add the cauliflower rice and cream cheese to the skillet. Cook for 7 minutes, stirring frequently, until the cream cheese melts and the cauliflower is tender. Remove the skillet from the heat and stir in the Cheddar cheese. Using a cookie scoop, form the mixture into 1½-inch balls. Place the balls on a parchment paper-lined baking sheet. Freeze for 30 minutes. Place the egg in a shallow bowl and beat it with a fork. In a separate bowl, stir together the almond flour and Parmesan cheese. Dip the cauliflower balls into the egg, then coat them with the almond flour mixture, gently pressing the mixture to the balls to adhere. Set the Ninja Foodi Multi-cooker to 205°C. Spray the cauliflower rice balls with oil, and arrange them in a single layer in the cook & crisp basket, working in batches if necessary. Air crisp for 5 minutes. Flip the rice balls and spray them with more oil. Air crisp for 3 to 7 minutes longer, until the balls are golden brown. Serve warm with marinara sauce.

Beef Tenderloin with Red Wine Sauce

Prep time: 30 minutes | Cook time: 10 minutes | Serves 5

900 g beef tenderloin
Salt and black pepper, to taste
2 tablespoons avocado oil
120 ml beef broth
120 ml dry red wine
2 cloves garlic, minced

1 teaspoon Worcestershire sauce
1½ teaspoons dried rosemary
¼ teaspoon xanthan gum
Chopped fresh rosemary, for garnish (optional)

Thirty minutes prior to cooking, take the tenderloin out of the fridge and let it come to room temperature. Crust the outside of the tenderloin in salt and pepper. Turn the pot to Sauté mode and add the avocado oil. Once hot, add the tenderloin and sear on all sides, about 5 minutes. Press Start/Stop. Add the broth, wine, garlic, Worcestershire sauce, and rosemary to the pot around the beef. Close the lid and seal the vent. Cook on High Pressure for 8 minutes. Quick release the steam. Remove the tenderloin to a platter, tent with aluminium foil, and let it rest for 10 minutes. Press Start/Stop. Turn the pot to Sauté mode. Once the broth has begun a low boil, add the xanthan gum and whisk until a thin sauce has formed, 2 to 3 minutes. Slice the tenderloin against the grain into thin rounds. Top each slice with the red wine glaze. Garnish with rosemary, if desired.

Tomato and Bacon Zoodles

Prep time: 10 minutes | Cook time: 15 to 22 minutes
| Serves 2

230 g sliced bacon
120 ml baby plum tomatoes
1 large courgette, spiralized
120 ml ricotta cheese
60 ml double/whipping cream

80 ml finely grated Parmesan cheese, plus more for serving
Sea salt and freshly ground black pepper, to taste

Set the Ninja Foodi Multi-cooker to 205°C. Arrange the bacon strips in a single layer in the cook & crisp basket—some overlapping is okay because the bacon will shrink, but cook in batches if needed. Air crisp for 8 minutes. Flip the bacon strips and air crisp for 2 to 5 minutes more, until the bacon is crisp. Remove the bacon from the Ninja Foodi Multi-cooker. Put the tomatoes in the cook & crisp basket and air crisp for 3 to 5 minutes, until they are just starting to burst. Remove the tomatoes from the Ninja Foodi Multi-cooker. Put the courgette noodles in the Ninja Foodi Multi-cooker and air crisp for 2 to 4 minutes, to the desired doneness. Meanwhile, combine the ricotta, cream, and Parmesan in a saucepan over medium-low heat. Cook, stirring often, until warm and combined. Crumble the bacon. Place the courgette, bacon, and tomatoes in a bowl. Toss with the ricotta sauce. Season with salt and pepper, and sprinkle with additional Parmesan.

Beef Whirls

Prep time: 30 minutes | Cook time: 18 minutes | Serves 6

3 minute steaks (170 g each)
1 (450 g) bottle Italian dressing
235 ml Italian-style bread crumbs (or plain bread crumbs with Italian seasoning to taste)
120 ml grated Parmesan cheese
1 teaspoon dried basil
1 teaspoon dried oregano
1 teaspoon dried parsley
60 ml beef stock
1 to 2 tablespoons oil

In a large resealable bag, combine the steaks and Italian dressing. Seal the bag and refrigerate to marinate for 2 hours. In a medium bowl, whisk the bread crumbs, cheese, basil, oregano, and parsley until blended. Stir in the beef stock. Place the steaks on a cutting board and cut each in half so you have 6 equal pieces. Sprinkle with the bread crumb mixture. Roll up the steaks, jelly roll-style, and secure with toothpicks. Preheat the Ninja Foodi Multi-cooker to 205°C. Place 3 roll-ups in the cook & crisp basket. Cook for 5 minutes. Flip the roll-ups and spritz with oil. Cook for 4 minutes more until the internal temperature reaches 65°C. Repeat with the remaining roll-ups. Let rest for 5 to 10 minutes before serving.

Garlic-Marinated Bavette Steak

Prep time: 30 minutes | Cook time: 8 to 10 minutes | Serves 6

120 ml avocado oil
60 ml soy sauce or tamari
1 shallot, minced
1 tablespoon minced garlic
2 tablespoons chopped fresh oregano, or 2 teaspoons dried
1½ teaspoons sea salt
1 teaspoon freshly ground black pepper
¼ teaspoon red pepper flakes
900 g bavette or skirt steak

In a blender, combine the avocado oil, soy sauce, shallot, garlic, oregano, salt, black pepper, and red pepper flakes. Process until smooth. Place the steak in a zip-top plastic bag or shallow dish with the marinade. Seal the bag or cover the dish and marinate in the refrigerator for at least 2 hours or overnight. Remove the steak from the bag and discard the marinade. Set the Ninja Foodi Multi-cooker to 205°C. Place the steak in the cook & crisp basket (if needed, cut into sections and work in batches). Air crisp for 4 to 6 minutes, flip the steak, and cook for another 4 minutes or until the internal temperature reaches 49°C in the thickest part for medium-rare (or as desired).

Tuscan Air Fried Veal Loin

Prep time: 1 hour 10 minutes | Cook time: 12 minutes | Makes 3 veal chops

1½ teaspoons crushed fennel seeds
1 tablespoon minced fresh rosemary leaves
1 tablespoon minced garlic
1½ teaspoons lemon zest
1½ teaspoons salt
½ teaspoon red pepper flakes
2 tablespoons olive oil
3 (280 g) bone-in veal loin, about ½ inch thick

Combine all the ingredients, except for the veal loin, in a large bowl. Stir to mix well. Dunk the loin in the mixture and press to submerge. Wrap the bowl in plastic and refrigerate for at least an hour to marinate. Preheat the Ninja Foodi Multi-cooker to 205°C. Arrange the veal loin in the preheated Ninja Foodi Multi-cooker and air crisp for 12 minutes for medium-rare, or until it reaches your desired doneness. Serve immediately.

Panko Crusted Calf's Liver Strips

Prep time: 15 minutes | Cook time: 23 to 25 minutes | Serves 4

450 g sliced calf's liver, cut into ½-inch wide strips
2 eggs
2 tablespoons milk
120 ml whole wheat flour
475 ml panko breadcrumbs
Salt and ground black pepper, to taste
Cooking spray

Preheat the Ninja Foodi Multi-cooker to 200°C and spritz with cooking spray. Rub the calf's liver strips with salt and ground black pepper on a clean work surface. Whisk the eggs with milk in a large bowl. Pour the flour in a shallow dish. Pour the panko on a separate shallow dish. Dunk the liver strips in the flour, then in the egg mixture. Shake the excess off and roll the strips over the panko to coat well. Arrange half of the liver strips in a single layer in the preheated Ninja Foodi Multi-cooker and spritz with cooking spray. Air crisp for 5 minutes or until browned. Flip the strips halfway through. Repeat with the remaining strips. Serve immediately.

Chapter 7 Vegetables and Sides

Chapter 7 Vegetables and Sides

Chermoula-Roasted Beetroots

Prep time: 15 minutes | Cook time: 25 minutes | Serves 4

Chermoula:
30 g packed fresh coriander leaves
15 g packed fresh parsley leaves
6 cloves garlic, peeled
2 teaspoons smoked paprika
2 teaspoons ground cumin
1 teaspoon ground coriander
½ to 1 teaspoon cayenne pepper
Pinch crushed saffron (optional)

115 ml extra-virgin olive oil
coarse sea salt, to taste
Beetroots:
3 medium beetroots, trimmed, peeled, and cut into 1-inch chunks
2 tablespoons chopped fresh coriander
2 tablespoons chopped fresh parsley

For the chermoula: In a food processor, combine the fresh coriander, parsley, garlic, paprika, cumin, ground coriander, and cayenne. Pulse until coarsely chopped. Add the saffron, if using, and process until combined. With the food processor running, slowly add the olive oil in a steady stream; process until the sauce is uniform. Season to taste with salt. For the beetroots: In a large bowl, drizzle the beetroots with ½ cup of the chermoula, or enough to coat. Arrange the beetroots in the cook & crisp basket. Set the Ninja Foodi Multi-cooker to 190°C for 25 to minutes, or until the beetroots are tender. Transfer the beetroots to a serving platter. Sprinkle with chopped coriander and parsley and serve.

Parmesan-Rosemary Radishes

Prep time: 5 minutes | Cook time: 15 to 20 minutes | Serves 4

1 bunch radishes, stemmed, trimmed, and quartered
1 tablespoon avocado oil
2 tablespoons finely grated fresh Parmesan cheese

1 tablespoon chopped fresh rosemary
Sea salt and freshly ground black pepper, to taste

Place the radishes in a medium bowl and toss them with the avocado oil, Parmesan cheese, rosemary, salt, and pepper. Set the Ninja Foodi Multi-cooker to190°C. Arrange the radishes in a single layer in the cook & crisp basket. Roast for 15 to 20 minutes, until golden brown and tender. Let cool for 5 minutes before serving.

Gobi Masala

Prep time: 5 minutes | Cook time: 4 to 5 minutes | Serves 4 to 6

1 tablespoon olive oil
1 teaspoon cumin seeds
1 white onion, diced
1 garlic clove, minced
1 head cauliflower, chopped

1 tablespoon ground coriander
1 teaspoon ground cumin
½ teaspoon garam masala
½ teaspoon salt
240 ml water

Set the Ninja Foodi Multi-cooker to the Sauté mode and heat the olive oil. Add the cumin seeds to the pot and sauté for 30 seconds, stirring constantly. Add the onion and sauté for 2 to 3 minutes, stirring constantly. Add the garlic and sauté for 30 seconds, stirring frequently. Stir in the remaining ingredients. Lock the lid. Set the cooking time for 1 minute on High Pressure. When the timer goes off, perform a quick pressure release. Carefully open the lid. Serve immediately.

Broccoli-Cheddar Twice-Baked Potatoes

Prep time: 10 minutes | Cook time: 46 minutes | Serves 4

Oil, for spraying
2 medium Maris Piper potatoes
1 tablespoon olive oil
30 g broccoli florets

1 tablespoon sour cream
1 teaspoon garlic powder
1 teaspoon onion powder
60 g shredded Cheddar cheese

Line the cook & crisp basket with parchment and spray lightly with oil. Rinse the potatoes and pat dry with paper towels. Rub the outside of the potatoes with the olive oil and place them in the prepared basket. Air crisp at 200°C for 40 minutes, or until easily pierced with a fork. Let cool just enough to handle, then cut the potatoes in half lengthwise. Meanwhile, place the broccoli in a microwave-safe bowl, cover with water, and microwave on high for 5 to 8 minutes. Drain and set aside. Scoop out most of the potato flesh and transfer to a medium bowl. Add the sour cream, garlic, and onion powder and stir until the potatoes are mashed. Spoon the potato mixture back into the hollowed potato skins, mounding it to fit, if necessary. Top with the broccoli and cheese. Return the potatoes to the basket. You may need to work in batches, depending on the size of your Ninja Foodi Multi-cooker. Air crisp at 200°C for 3 to 6 minutes, or until the cheese has melted. Serve immediately.

Mediterranean Courgette Boats

Prep time: 5 minutes | Cook time: 10 minutes | Serves 4

1 large courgette, ends removed, halved lengthwise	65 g feta cheese
6 grape tomatoes, quartered	1 tablespoon balsamic vinegar
¼ teaspoon salt	1 tablespoon olive oil

Use a spoon to scoop out 2 tablespoons from centre of each courgette half, making just enough space to fill with tomatoes and feta. Place tomatoes evenly in centres of courgette halves and sprinkle with salt. Place into ungreased cook & crisp basket. Adjust the temperature to 180°C and roast for 10 minutes. When done, courgette will be tender. Transfer boats to a serving tray and sprinkle with feta, then drizzle with vinegar and olive oil. Serve warm.

Fig, Chickpea, and Rocket Salad

Prep time: 15 minutes | Cook time: 20 minutes | Serves 4

8 fresh figs, halved	2 tablespoons extra-virgin olive oil, plus more for greasing
250 g cooked chickpeas	
1 teaspoon crushed roasted cumin seeds	Salt and ground black pepper, to taste
4 tablespoons balsamic vinegar	40 g rocket, washed and dried

Preheat the Ninja Foodi Multi-cooker to 190°C. Cover the cook & crisp basket with aluminum foil and grease lightly with oil. Put the figs in the cook & crisp basket and air crisp for 10 minutes. In a bowl, combine the chickpeas and cumin seeds. Remove the air fried figs from the Ninja Foodi Multi-cooker and replace with the chickpeas. Air crisp for 10 minutes. Leave to cool. In the meantime, prepare the dressing. Mix the balsamic vinegar, olive oil, salt and pepper. In a salad bowl, combine the rocket with the cooled figs and chickpeas. Toss with the sauce and serve.

Roasted Brussels Sprouts with Bacon

Prep time: 10 minutes | Cook time: 20 minutes | Serves 4

4 slices thick-cut bacon, chopped (about 110 g)	(or quartered if large)
450 g Brussels sprouts, halved	Freshly ground black pepper, to taste

Preheat the Ninja Foodi Multi-cooker to 190°C. Air crisp the bacon for 5 minutes, shaking the basket once or twice during the cooking time. Add the Brussels sprouts to the basket and drizzle a little bacon fat from the bottom of the Ninja Foodi Multi-cooker drawer into the basket. Toss the sprouts to coat with the bacon fat. Air crisp for an additional 15 minutes, or until the Brussels sprouts are tender to a knifepoint. Season with freshly ground black pepper.

Green Beans with Potatoes and Basil

Prep time: 20 minutes | Cook time: 10 minutes | Serves 4

2 tablespoons extra-virgin olive oil, plus extra for drizzling	1 teaspoon table salt
	¼ teaspoon pepper
1 onion, chopped fine	680 g green beans, trimmed and cut into 2-inch lengths
2 tablespoons minced fresh oregano or 2 teaspoons dried	450 g Yukon Gold potatoes, peeled and cut into 1-inch pieces
2 tablespoons tomato paste	
4 garlic cloves, minced	3 tablespoons chopped fresh basil or parsley
1 (410 g) can whole peeled tomatoes, drained with juice reserved, chopped	2 tablespoons toasted pine nuts
240 ml water	Shaved Parmesan cheese

Using highest sauté function, heat oil in Ninja Foodi Multi-cooker until shimmering. Add onion and cook until softened, about 5 minutes. Stir in oregano, tomato paste, and garlic and cook until fragrant, about 30 seconds. Stir in tomatoes and their juice, water, salt, and pepper, then stir in green beans and potatoes. Lock lid in place and close pressure release valve. Select high pressure cook function and cook for 5 minutes. Turn off Ninja Foodi Multi-cooker and quick-release pressure. Carefully remove lid, allowing steam to escape away from you. Season with salt and pepper to taste. Sprinkle individual portions with basil, pine nuts, and Parmesan and drizzle with extra oil. Serve.

Asian Tofu Salad

Prep time: 25 minutes | Cook time: 15 minutes | Serves 2

Tofu:	1 tablespoon sugar
1 tablespoon soy sauce	1 teaspoon salt
1 tablespoon vegetable oil	1 teaspoon black pepper
1 teaspoon minced fresh ginger	25 g sliced spring onions
1 teaspoon minced garlic	120 g julienned cucumber
230 g extra-firm tofu, drained and cubed	50 g julienned red onion
	130 g julienned carrots
Salad:	6 butter lettuce leaves
60 ml rice vinegar	

For the tofu: In a small bowl, whisk together the soy sauce, vegetable oil, ginger, and garlic. Add the tofu and mix gently. Let stand at room temperature for 10 minutes. Arrange the tofu in a single layer in the cook & crisp basket. Set the Ninja Foodi Multi-cooker to 200°C for 15 minutes, shaking halfway through the cooking time. Meanwhile, for the salad: In a large bowl, whisk together the vinegar, sugar, salt, pepper, and spring onions. Add the cucumber, onion, and carrots and toss to combine. Set aside to marinate while the tofu cooks. To serve, arrange three lettuce leaves on each of two plates. Pile the marinated vegetables (and marinade) on the lettuce. Divide the tofu between the plates and serve.

Parmesan and Herb Sweet Potatoes

Prep time: 10 minutes | Cook time: 18 minutes | Serves 4

2 large sweet potatoes, peeled and cubed	½ teaspoon salt
65 ml olive oil	2 tablespoons shredded Parmesan
1 teaspoon dried rosemary	

Preheat the Ninja Foodi Multi-cooker to 180°C. In a large bowl, toss the sweet potatoes with the olive oil, rosemary, and salt. Pour the potatoes into the cook & crisp basket and roast for 10 minutes, then stir the potatoes and sprinkle the Parmesan over the top. Continue roasting for 8 minutes more. Serve hot and enjoy.

Lemon-Thyme Asparagus

Prep time: 5 minutes | Cook time: 4 to 8 minutes | Serves 4

450 g asparagus, woody ends trimmed off	Sea salt and freshly ground black pepper, to taste
1 tablespoon avocado oil	60 g goat cheese, crumbled
½ teaspoon dried thyme or ½ tablespoon chopped fresh thyme	Zest and juice of 1 lemon
	Flaky sea salt, for serving (optional)

In a medium bowl, toss together the asparagus, avocado oil, and thyme, and season with sea salt and pepper. Place the asparagus in the cook & crisp basket in a single layer. Set the Ninja Foodi Multi-cooker to 200°C and air crisp for 4 to 8 minutes, to your desired doneness. Transfer to a serving platter. Top with the goat cheese, lemon zest, and lemon juice. If desired, season with a pinch of flaky salt.

"Faux-Tato" Hash

Prep time: 10 minutes | Cook time: 12 minutes | Serves 4

450 g radishes, ends removed, quartered	2 tablespoons salted butter, melted
¼ medium yellow onion, peeled and diced	½ teaspoon garlic powder
½ medium green pepper, seeded and chopped	¼ teaspoon ground black pepper

In a large bowl, combine radishes, onion, and bell pepper. Toss with butter. Sprinkle garlic powder and black pepper over mixture in bowl, then spoon into ungreased cook & crisp basket. Adjust the temperature to 160°C and air crisp for 12 minutes. Shake basket halfway through cooking. Radishes will be tender when done. Serve warm.

Chinese-Style Pe-Tsai with Onion

Prep time: 5 minutes | Cook time: 8 minutes | Serves 4

2 tablespoons sesame oil	1 tablespoon coconut aminos
1 brown onion, chopped	1 teaspoon finely minced garlic
450 g pe-tsai cabbage, shredded	½ teaspoon salt
60 ml rice wine vinegar	¼ teaspoon Szechuan pepper

Set the Ninja Foodi Multi-cooker on the Sauté mode and heat the sesame oil. Add the onion to the pot and sauté for 5 minutes, or until tender. Stir in the remaining ingredients. Lock the lid. Set the cooking time for 3 minutes on High Pressure. When the timer goes off, perform a quick pressure release. Carefully open the lid. Transfer the cabbage mixture to a bowl and serve immediately.

Parsnip Fries with Romesco Sauce

Prep time: 20 minutes | Cook time: 24 minutes | Serves 4

Romesco Sauce:	seeded
1 red pepper, halved and seeded	1 tablespoon red wine vinegar
1 (1-inch) thick slice of Italian bread, torn into pieces	¼ teaspoon smoked paprika
130 g almonds, toasted	½ teaspoon salt
Olive oil	180 ml olive oil
½ Jalapeño pepper, seeded	3 parsnips, peeled and cut into long strips
1 tablespoon fresh parsley leaves	2 teaspoons olive oil
1 clove garlic	Salt and freshly ground black pepper, to taste
2 plum tomatoes, peeled and	

Preheat the Ninja Foodi Multi-cooker to 200°C. Place the red pepper halves, cut side down, in the cook & crisp basket and air crisp for 8 to 10 minutes, or until the skin turns black all over. Remove the pepper from the Ninja Foodi Multi-cooker and let it cool. When it is cool enough to handle, peel the pepper. Toss the torn bread and almonds with a little olive oil and air crisp for 4 minutes, shaking the basket a couple times throughout the cooking time. When the bread and almonds are nicely toasted, remove them from the Ninja Foodi Multi-cooker and let them cool for just a minute or two. Combine the toasted bread, almonds, roasted red pepper, Jalapeño pepper, parsley, garlic, tomatoes, vinegar, smoked paprika and salt in a food processor or blender. Process until smooth. With the processor running, add the olive oil through the feed tube until the sauce comes together in a smooth paste that is barely pourable. Toss the parsnip strips with the olive oil, salt and freshly ground black pepper and air crisp at 200°C for 10 minutes, shaking the basket a couple times during the cooking process so they brown and cook evenly. Serve the parsnip fries warm with the Romesco sauce to dip into.

Dijon Roast Cabbage

Prep time: 10 minutes | Cook time: 10 minutes | Serves 4

1 small head cabbage, cored and sliced into 1-inch-thick slices	½ teaspoon salt
	1 tablespoon Dijon mustard
2 tablespoons olive oil, divided	1 teaspoon apple cider vinegar
	1 teaspoon granular erythritol

Drizzle each cabbage slice with 1 tablespoon olive oil, then sprinkle with salt. Place slices into ungreased cook & crisp basket, working in batches if needed. Adjust the temperature to 180ºC and air crisp for 10 minutes. Cabbage will be tender and edges will begin to brown when done. In a small bowl, whisk remaining olive oil with mustard, vinegar, and erythritol. Drizzle over cabbage in a large serving dish. Serve warm.

Garlic Cauliflower with Tahini

Prep time: 10 minutes | Cook time: 20 minutes | Serves 4

Cauliflower:	½ teaspoon coarse sea salt
500 g cauliflower florets (about 1 large head)	Sauce:
	2 tablespoons tahini (sesame paste)
6 garlic cloves, smashed and cut into thirds	
3 tablespoons vegetable oil	2 tablespoons hot water
	1 tablespoon fresh lemon juice
½ teaspoon ground cumin	1 teaspoon minced garlic
½ teaspoon ground coriander	½ teaspoon coarse sea salt

For the cauliflower: In a large bowl, combine the cauliflower florets and garlic. Drizzle with the vegetable oil. Sprinkle with the cumin, coriander, and salt. Toss until well coated. Place the cauliflower in the cook & crisp basket. Set the Ninja Foodi Multi-cooker to 200ºC for 20 minutes, turning the cauliflower halfway through the cooking time. Meanwhile, for the sauce: In a small bowl, combine the tahini, water, lemon juice, garlic, and salt. (The sauce will appear curdled at first, but keep stirring until you have a thick, creamy, smooth mixture.) Transfer the cauliflower to a large serving bowl. Pour the sauce over and toss gently to coat. Serve immediately.

Simple Cauliflower Gnocchi

Prep time: 5 minutes | Cook time: 2 minutes | Serves 4

480 ml cauliflower, boiled	1 teaspoon salt
120 ml almond flour	240 ml water
1 tablespoon sesame oil	

In a bowl, mash the cauliflower until puréed. Mix it up with the almond flour, sesame oil and salt. Make the log from the cauliflower dough and cut it into small pieces. Pour the water in the Ninja Foodi Multi-cooker and add the gnocchi. Lock the lid. Set the cooking time for 2 minutes on High Pressure. Once the timer goes off, perform a natural pressure release for 5 minutes, then release any remaining pressure. Carefully open the lid. Remove the cooked gnocchi from the water and serve.

Courgette and Daikon Fritters

Prep time: 10 minutes | Cook time: 8 minutes | Serves 4

2 large courgettes, grated	1 teaspoon ground flax meal
1 daikon, diced	1 teaspoon salt
1 egg, beaten	1 tablespoon coconut oil

In the mixing bowl, combine all the ingredients, except for the coconut oil. Form the courgette mixture into fritters. Press the Sauté button on the Ninja Foodi Multi-cooker and melt the coconut oil. Place the courgette fritters in the hot oil and cook for 4 minutes on each side, or until golden brown. Transfer to a plate and serve.

Perfect Sweet Potatoes

Prep time: 5 minutes | Cook time: 15 minutes |
Serves 4 to 6

4–6 medium sweet potatoes	240 ml of water

Scrub skin of sweet potatoes with a brush until clean. Pour water into inner pot of the Ninja Foodi Multi-cooker. Place steamer basket in the bottom of the inner pot. Place sweet potatoes on top of steamer basket. Secure the lid and turn valve to seal. Set to pressure cook on high for 15 minutes. Allow pressure to release naturally (about 10 minutes). Once the pressure valve lowers, remove lid and serve immediately.

Tahini-Lemon Kale

Prep time: 5 minutes | Cook time: 15 minutes |
Serves 2 to 4

60 g tahini	110 g packed torn kale leaves (stems and ribs removed and leaves torn into palm-size pieces)
60 ml fresh lemon juice	
2 tablespoons olive oil	
1 teaspoon sesame seeds	
½ teaspoon garlic powder	coarse sea salt and freshly ground black pepper, to taste
¼ teaspoon cayenne pepper	

In a large bowl, whisk together the tahini, lemon juice, olive oil, sesame seeds, garlic powder, and cayenne until smooth. Add the kale leaves, season with salt and black pepper, and toss in the dressing until completely coated. Transfer the kale leaves to a cake pan. Place the pan in the Ninja Foodi Multi-cooker and roast at 180ºC, stirring every 5 minutes, until the kale is wilted and the top is lightly browned, about 15 minutes. Remove the pan from the Ninja Foodi Multi-cooker and serve warm.

Wild Rice Salad with Cranberries and Almonds

Prep time: 10 minutes | Cook time: 25 minutes | Serves 18

For the rice
480 ml wild rice blend, rinsed
1 teaspoon rock salt
600 ml Vegetable Broth or
Chicken Bone Broth
For the dressing
60 ml extra-virgin olive oil
60 ml white wine vinegar
1½ teaspoons grated orange
zest

Juice of 1 medium orange
(about 60 ml)
1 teaspoon honey or pure maple
syrup
For the salad
180 ml unsweetened dried
cranberries
120 ml sliced almonds, toasted
Freshly ground black pepper

Make the Rice In the electric pressure cooker, combine the rice, salt, and broth. Close and lock the lid. Set the valve to sealing. Cook on high pressure for 25 minutes. When the cooking is complete, hit Start/Stop and allow the pressure to release naturally for 15 minutes, then quick release any remaining pressure. Once the pin drops, unlock and remove the lid. Let the rice cool briefly, then fluff it with a fork. Make the Dressing While the rice cooks, make the dressing: In a small jar with a screw-top lid, combine the olive oil, vinegar, zest, juice, and honey. (If you don't have a jar, whisk the ingredients together in a small bowl.) Shake to combine. Make the Salad In a large bowl, combine the rice, cranberries, and almonds. Add the dressing and season with pepper. Serve warm or refrigerate.

Braised Fennel with radicchio, Pear, and Pecorino

Prep time: 20 minutes | Cook time: 12 minutes | Serves 4

6 tablespoons extra-virgin olive
oil, divided
2 fennel bulbs (340 g each), 2
tablespoons fronds chopped,
stalks discarded, bulbs halved,
each half cut into 1-inch-thick
wedges
¾ teaspoon table salt, divided
½ teaspoon grated lemon zest
plus 4 teaspoons juice

140 g baby rocket
1 small head radicchio (170 g),
shredded
1 Bosc or Bartlett pear,
quartered, cored, and sliced thin
60 ml whole almonds, toasted
and chopped
Shaved Pecorino Romano
cheese

Using highest sauté function, heat 2 tablespoons oil in Ninja Foodi Multi-cooker for 5 minutes (or until just smoking). Brown half of fennel, about 3 minutes per side; transfer to plate. Repeat with 1 tablespoon oil and remaining fennel; do not remove from pot. Return first batch of fennel to pot along with 120 ml water and ½ teaspoon salt. Lock lid in place and close pressure release valve.

Select high pressure cook function and cook for 2 minutes. Turn off Ninja Foodi Multi-cooker and quick-release pressure. Carefully remove lid, allowing steam to escape away from you. Using slotted spoon, transfer fennel to plate; discard cooking liquid. Whisk remaining 3 tablespoons oil, lemon zest and juice, and remaining ¼ teaspoon salt together in large bowl. Add rocket, radicchio, and pear and toss to coat. Transfer rocket mixture to serving dish and arrange fennel wedges on top. Sprinkle with almonds, fennel fronds, and Pecorino. Serve.

Sesame Carrots and Sugar Snap Peas

Prep time: 10 minutes | Cook time: 16 minutes | Serves 4

450 g carrots, peeled sliced on
the bias (½-inch slices)
1 teaspoon olive oil
Salt and freshly ground black
pepper, to taste
110 g honey

1 tablespoon sesame oil
1 tablespoon soy sauce
½ teaspoon minced fresh ginger
110 g sugar snap peas
1½ teaspoons sesame seeds

Preheat the Ninja Foodi Multi-cooker to 180°C. Toss the carrots with the olive oil, season with salt and pepper and air crisp for 10 minutes, shaking the basket once or twice during the cooking process. Combine the honey, sesame oil, soy sauce and minced ginger in a large bowl. Add the sugar snap peas and the air-fried carrots to the honey mixture, toss to coat and return everything to the cook & crisp basket. Turn up the temperature to 200°C and air crisp for an additional 6 minutes, shaking the basket once during the cooking process. Transfer the carrots and sugar snap peas to a serving bowl. Pour the sauce from the bottom of the cooker over the vegetables and sprinkle sesame seeds over top. Serve immediately.

Baked Jalapeño and Cheese Cauliflower Mash

Prep time: 10 minutes | Cook time: 15 minutes | Serves 6

1 (340 g) steamer bag
cauliflower florets, cooked
according to package
instructions
2 tablespoons salted butter,
softened
60 g cream cheese, softened

120 g shredded sharp Cheddar
cheese
20 g pickled jalapeños
½ teaspoon salt
¼ teaspoon ground black
pepper

Place cooked cauliflower into a food processor with remaining ingredients. Pulse twenty times until cauliflower is smooth and all ingredients are combined. Spoon mash into an ungreased round nonstick baking dish. Place dish into cook & crisp basket. Adjust the temperature to 190°C and bake for 15 minutes. The top will be golden brown when done. Serve warm.

Braised Whole Cauliflower with North African Spices

Prep time: 15 minutes | Cook time: 10 minutes | Serves 4

2 tablespoons extra-virgin olive oil

6 garlic cloves, minced

3 anchovy fillets, rinsed and minced (optional)

2 teaspoons ras el hanout

⅛ teaspoon red pepper flakes

1 (800 g) can whole peeled tomatoes, drained with juice reserved, chopped coarse

1 large head cauliflower (about 1.4 kg)

120 ml pitted brine-cured green olives, chopped coarse

60 ml golden raisins

60 ml fresh coriander leaves

60 ml pine nuts, toasted

Using highest sauté function, cook oil, garlic, anchovies (if using), ras el hanout, and pepper flakes in Ninja Foodi Multi-cooker until fragrant, about 3 minutes. Turn off Ninja Foodi Multi-cooker, then stir in tomatoes and reserved juice. Trim outer leaves of cauliflower and cut stem flush with bottom florets. Using paring knife, cut 4-inch-deep cross in stem. Nestle cauliflower stem side down into pot and spoon some of sauce over top. Lock lid in place and close pressure release valve. Select high pressure cook function and cook for 3 minutes. Turn off Ninja Foodi Multi-cooker and quick-release pressure. Carefully remove lid, allowing steam to escape away from you. Using tongs and slotted spoon, transfer cauliflower to serving dish and tent with aluminium foil. Stir olives and raisins into sauce and cook, using highest sauté function, until sauce has thickened slightly, about 5 minutes. Season with salt and pepper to taste. Cut cauliflower into wedges and spoon some of sauce over top. Sprinkle with coriander and pine nuts. Serve, passing remaining sauce separately.

Curried Cauliflower and Tomatoes

Prep time: 10 minutes | Cook time: 2 minutes | Serves 4 to 6

1 medium head cauliflower, cut into bite-size pieces

1 (400 g) can sugar-free diced tomatoes, undrained

1 bell pepper, thinly sliced

1 (400 g) can full-fat coconut milk

½ to 240 ml water

2 tablespoons red curry paste

1 teaspoon salt

1 teaspoon garlic powder

½ teaspoon onion powder

½ teaspoon ground ginger

¼ teaspoon chili powder

Freshly ground black pepper, to taste

Add all the ingredients, except for the black pepper, to the Ninja Foodi Multi-cooker and stir to combine. Lock the lid. Set the cooking time for 2 minutes at High Pressure. Once the timer goes off, use a quick pressure release. Carefully open the lid. Sprinkle the black pepper and stir well. Serve immediately.

Spinach and Sweet Pepper Poppers

Prep time: 10 minutes | Cook time: 8 minutes | Makes 16 poppers

110 g cream cheese, softened

20 g chopped fresh spinach leaves

½ teaspoon garlic powder

8 mini sweet bell peppers, tops removed, seeded, and halved lengthwise

In a medium bowl, mix cream cheese, spinach, and garlic powder. Place 1 tablespoon mixture into each sweet pepper half and press down to smooth. Place poppers into ungreased cook & crisp basket. Adjust the temperature to 200°C and air crisp for 8 minutes. Poppers will be done when cheese is browned on top and peppers are tender-crisp. Serve warm.

Stir Fried Asparagus and Kale

Prep time: 5 minutes | Cook time: 3 minutes | Serves 4

230 g asparagus, chopped

480 ml chopped kale

2 bell peppers, chopped

1 tablespoon avocado oil

1 teaspoon apple cider vinegar

½ teaspoon minced ginger

120 ml water

Pour the water into the Ninja Foodi Multi-cooker. In the Ninja Foodi Multi-cooker pan, stir together the remaining ingredients. Insert the trivet and place the pan on it. Set the lid in place. Set the cooking time for 3 minutes on High Pressure. When the timer goes off, perform a quick pressure release. Carefully open the lid. Serve immediately.

Butternut Squash Croquettes

Prep time: 5 minutes | Cook time: 17 minutes | Serves 4

⅓ butternut squash, peeled and grated

40 g plain flour

2 eggs, whisked

4 cloves garlic, minced

1½ tablespoons olive oil

1 teaspoon fine sea salt

⅓ teaspoon freshly ground black pepper, or more to taste

⅓ teaspoon dried sage

A pinch of ground allspice

Preheat the Ninja Foodi Multi-cooker to 170°C. Line the cook & crisp basket with parchment paper. In a mixing bowl, stir together all the ingredients until well combined. Make the squash croquettes: Use a small cookie scoop to drop tablespoonfuls of the squash mixture onto a lightly floured surface and shape into balls with your hands. Transfer them to the cook & crisp basket. Air crisp for 17 minutes until the squash croquettes are golden brown. Remove from the basket to a plate and serve warm.

Individual Asparagus and Goat Cheese Frittatas

Prep time: 15 minutes | Cook time: 15 minutes | Serves 4

1 tablespoon extra-virgin olive oil

230 g asparagus, trimmed and sliced ¼ inch thick

1 red bell pepper, stemmed, seeded, and chopped

2 shallots, minced

60 g goat cheese, crumbled (120 ml)

1 tablespoon minced fresh tarragon

1 teaspoon grated lemon zest

8 large eggs

½ teaspoon table salt

Using highest sauté function, heat oil in Ninja Foodi Multi-cooker until shimmering. Add asparagus, bell pepper, and shallots; cook until softened, about 5 minutes. Turn off Ninja Foodi Multi-cooker and transfer vegetables to bowl. Stir in goat cheese, tarragon, and lemon zest. Arrange trivet included with Ninja Foodi Multi-cooker in base of now-empty insert and add 240 ml water. Spray four 170-g ramekins with vegetable oil spray. Beat eggs, 60 ml water, and salt in large bowl until thoroughly combined. Divide vegetable mixture between prepared ramekins, then pour egg mixture over top (you may have some left over). Set ramekins on trivet. Lock lid in place and close pressure release valve. Select high pressure cook function and cook for 10 minutes. Turn off Ninja Foodi Multi-cooker and quick-release pressure. Carefully remove lid, allowing steam to escape away from you. Using tongs, transfer ramekins to wire rack and let cool slightly. Run paring knife around inside edge of ramekins to loosen frittatas, then invert onto individual serving plates. Serve.

Cabbage Wedges with Caraway Butter

Prep time: 30 minutes | Cook time: 35 to 40 minutes | Serves 6

1 tablespoon caraway seeds

110 g unsalted butter, at room temperature

½ teaspoon grated lemon zest

1 small head green or red cabbage, cut into 6 wedges

1 tablespoon avocado oil

½ teaspoon sea salt

¼ teaspoon freshly ground black pepper

Place the caraway seeds in a small dry skillet over medium-high heat. Toast the seeds for 2 to 3 minutes, then remove them from the heat and let cool. Lightly crush the seeds using a mortar and pestle or with the back of a knife. Place the butter in a small bowl and stir in the crushed caraway seeds and lemon zest. Form the butter into a log and wrap it in parchment paper or plastic wrap. Refrigerate for at least 1 hour or freeze for 20 minutes. Brush or spray the cabbage wedges with the avocado oil, and sprinkle with the salt and pepper. Set the Ninja Foodi Multi-cooker to190°C. Place the cabbage in a single layer in the cook & crisp basket and roast for 20 minutes. Flip and cook for 15 to 20 minutes more, until the cabbage is tender and lightly charred. Plate the cabbage and dot with caraway butter. Tent with foil for 5 minutes to melt the butter, and serve.

Almond Butter Courgette Noodles

Prep time: 10 minutes | Cook time: 4 minutes | Serves 4

2 tablespoons coconut oil

1 brown onion, chopped

2 courgette, julienned

240 ml shredded Chinese cabbage

2 garlic cloves, minced

2 tablespoons almond butter

Sea salt and freshly ground black pepper, to taste

1 teaspoon cayenne pepper

Press the Sauté button to heat up your Ninja Foodi Multi-cooker. Heat the coconut oil and sweat the onion for 2 minutes. Add the other ingredients. Secure the lid. Cook at High Pressure for 2 minutes. Once cooking is complete, use a quick pressure release; carefully remove the lid. Bon appétit!

Chapter 8 Desserts

Chapter 8 Desserts

Chocolate Croissants

Prep time: 5 minutes | Cook time: 24 minutes | Serves 8

1 sheet frozen puff pastry, thawed

100 g chocolate-hazelnut spread
1 large egg, beaten

On a lightly floured surface, roll puff pastry into a 14-inch square. Cut pastry into quarters to form 4 squares. Cut each square diagonally to form 8 triangles. Spread 2 teaspoons chocolate-hazelnut spread on each triangle; from wider end, roll up pastry. Brush egg on top of each roll. Preheat the Ninja Foodi Multi-cooker to 190ºC. Air crisp rolls in batches, 3 or 4 at a time, 8 minutes per batch, or until pastry is golden brown. Cool on a wire rack; serve while warm or at room temperature.

Cardamom Custard

Prep time: 10 minutes | Cook time: 25 minutes | Serves 2

240 ml whole milk
1 large egg
2 tablespoons granulated sugar, plus 1 teaspoon

¼ teaspoon vanilla bean paste or pure vanilla extract
¼ teaspoon ground cardamom, plus more for sprinkling

In a medium bowl, beat together the milk, egg, sugar, vanilla, and cardamom. Place two ramekins in the cook & crisp basket. Divide the mixture between the ramekins. Sprinkle lightly with cardamom. Cover each ramekin tightly with aluminum foil. Set the Ninja Foodi Multi-cooker to 175ºC and cook for 25 minutes, or until a toothpick inserted in the center comes out clean. Let the custards cool on a wire rack for 5 to 10 minutes. Serve warm or refrigerate until cold and serve chilled.

Protein Powder Doughnut Holes

Prep time: 25 minutes | Cook time: 6 minutes | Makes 12 holes

50 g blanched finely ground almond flour
60 g low-carb vanilla protein powder
100 g granulated sweetener

½ teaspoon baking powder
1 large egg
5 tablespoons unsalted butter, melted
½ teaspoon vanilla extract

Mix all ingredients in a large bowl. Place into the freezer for 20

minutes. Wet your hands with water and roll the dough into twelve balls. Cut a piece of baking paper to fit your cook & crisp basket. Working in batches as necessary, place doughnut holes into the cook & crisp basket on top of baking paper. Adjust the temperature to 190ºC and air crisp for 6 minutes. Flip doughnut holes halfway through the cooking time. Let cool completely before serving.

Chocolate Fondue

Prep time: 5 minutes | Cook time: 2 minutes | Serves 4

60 g unsweetened baking chocolate, finely chopped, divided
240 ml double cream, divided
80 ml sweetener, divided

Fine sea salt
240 ml cold water
Special Equipment:
Set of fondue forks or wooden skewers

Divide the chocolate, cream, and sweetener evenly among four ramekins. Add a pinch of salt to each one and stir well. Cover the ramekins with aluminium foil. Place a trivet in the bottom of your Ninja Foodi Multi-cooker and pour in the water. Place the ramekins on the trivet. Lock the lid. Set the cooking time for 2 minutes at High Pressure. When the timer beeps, perform a natural pressure release for 10 minutes. Carefully remove the lid. Use tongs to remove the ramekins from the pot. Use a fork to stir the fondue until smooth. Use immediately.

Chocolate Pecan Clusters

Prep time: 5 minutes | Cook time: 5 minutes | Makes 8 clusters

3 tablespoons butter
60 ml double cream
1 teaspoon vanilla extract

240 ml chopped pecans
60 ml low-carb chocolate chips

Press the Sauté button and add butter to Ninja Foodi Multi-cooker. Allow butter to melt and begin to turn golden brown. Once it begins to brown, immediately add double cream. Press the Start/Stop button. Add vanilla and chopped pecans to Ninja Foodi Multi-cooker. Allow to cool for 10 minutes, stirring occasionally. Spoon mixture onto parchment-lined baking sheet to form eight clusters, and scatter chocolate chips over clusters. Place in fridge to cool.

Chocolate Chip Pecan Biscotti

Prep time: 15 minutes | Cook time: 20 to 22 minutes | Serves 10

135 g finely ground blanched almond flour

¾ teaspoon baking powder

½ teaspoon xanthan gum

¼ teaspoon sea salt

3 tablespoons unsalted butter, at room temperature

35 g powdered sweetener

1 large egg, beaten

1 teaspoon pure vanilla extract

50 g chopped pecans

40 g organic chocolate chips,

Melted organic chocolate chips and chopped pecans, for topping (optional)

In a large bowl, combine the almond flour, baking powder, xanthan gum, and salt. Line a cake pan that fits inside your Ninja Foodi Multi-cooker with baking paper. In the bowl of a stand mixer, beat together the butter and powdered sweetener. Add the beaten egg and vanilla and beat for about 3 minutes. Add the almond flour mixture to the butter and egg mixture; beat until just combined. Stir in the pecans and chocolate chips. Transfer the dough to the prepared pan and press it into the bottom. Set the Ninja Foodi Multi-cooker to 165°C and bake for 12 minutes. Remove from the Ninja Foodi Multi-cooker and let cool for 15 minutes. Using a sharp knife, cut the cookie into thin strips, then return the strips to the cake pan with the bottom sides facing up. Set the Ninja Foodi Multi-cooker to 148°C. Bake for 8 to 10 minutes. Remove from the Ninja Foodi Multi-cooker and let cool completely on a wire rack. If desired, dip one side of each biscotti piece into melted chocolate chips, and top with chopped pecans.

Chickpea Brownies

Prep time: 10 minutes | Cook time: 20 minutes | Serves 6

Vegetable oil

425 g can chickpeas, drained and rinsed

4 large eggs

80 ml coconut oil, melted

80 ml honey

3 tablespoons unsweetened

cocoa powder

1 tablespoon espresso powder (optional)

1 teaspoon baking powder

1 teaspoon baking soda

80 g chocolate chips

Preheat the Ninja Foodi Multi-cooker to 165°C. Generously grease a baking pan with vegetable oil. In a blender or food processor, combine the chickpeas, eggs, coconut oil, honey, cocoa powder, espresso powder (if using), baking powder, and baking soda. Blend or process until smooth. Transfer to the prepared pan and stir in the chocolate chips by hand. Set the pan in the cook & crisp basket and bake for 20 minutes, or until a toothpick inserted into the center comes out clean. Let cool in the pan on a wire rack for 30 minutes before cutting into squares. Serve immediately.

Pecan Clusters

Prep time: 10 minutes | Cook time: 8 minutes | Serves 8

85 g whole shelled pecans

1 tablespoon salted butter, melted

2 teaspoons powdered

sweetener

½ teaspoon ground cinnamon

½ cup low-carb chocolate chips

In a medium bowl, toss pecans with butter, then sprinkle with sweetener and cinnamon. Place pecans into ungreased cook & crisp basket. Adjust the temperature to 175°C and air crisp for 8 minutes, shaking the basket two times during cooking. They will feel soft initially but get crunchy as they cool. Line a large baking sheet with baking paper. Place chocolate in a medium microwave-safe bowl. Microwave on high, heating in 20-second increments and stirring until melted. Place 1 teaspoon chocolate in a rounded mound on ungreased baking paper -lined baking sheet, then press 1 pecan into top, repeating with remaining chocolate and pecans. Place baking sheet into refrigerator to cool at least 30 minutes. Once cooled, store clusters in a large, sealed container in refrigerator up to 5 days.

Pecan Pumpkin Pie

Prep time: 5 minutes | Cook time: 40 minutes | Serves 5 to 6

Base:

2 tablespoons grass-fed butter, softened

240 ml blanched almond flour

120 ml chopped pecans

Topping:

120 ml sweetener, or more to taste

80 ml heavy whipping cream

½ teaspoon ground cinnamon

½ teaspoon ginger, finely grated

½ teaspoon ground nutmeg

½ teaspoon ground cloves

1 (400 g) can organic pumpkin purée

1 egg

Pour 240 ml of filtered water into the inner pot of the Ninja Foodi Multi-cooker, then insert the trivet. Using an electric mixer, combine the butter, almond flour, and pecans. Mix thoroughly. Transfer this mixture into a well-greased, Ninja Foodi Multi-cooker-friendly pan, and form a crust at the bottom of the pan, with a slight coating of the mixture also on the sides. Freeze for 15 minutes. In a large bowl, thoroughly combine the topping ingredients. Take the pan from the freezer, add the topping evenly, and then place the pan onto the trivet. Cover loosely with aluminium foil. Close the lid, set the pressure release to Sealing. Set the Ninja Foodi Multi-cooker to 40 minutes on High Pressure, and let cook. Once cooked, let the pressure naturally disperse from the Ninja Foodi Multi-cooker for about 10 minutes, then carefully switch the pressure release to Venting. Open the Ninja Foodi Multi-cooker and remove the pan. Cool in the refrigerator for 4 to 5 hours, serve, and enjoy!

Vanilla Cookies with Hazelnuts

Prep time: 20 minutes | Cook time: 10 minutes | Serves 6

110 g almond flour
55 g coconut flour
1 teaspoon baking soda
1 teaspoon fine sea salt
110 g unsalted butter

120 g powdered sweetener
2 teaspoons vanilla
2 eggs, at room temperature
130 g hazelnuts, coarsely
chopped

Preheat the Ninja Foodi Multi-cooker to 175ºC. Mix the flour with the baking soda, and sea salt. In the bowl of an electric mixer, beat the butter, sweetener, and vanilla until creamy. Fold in the eggs, one at a time, and mix until well combined. Slowly and gradually, stir in the flour mixture. Finally, fold in the coarsely chopped hazelnuts. Divide the dough into small balls using a large cookie scoop; drop onto the prepared cookie sheets. Bake for 10 minutes or until golden brown, rotating the pan once or twice through the cooking time. Work in batches and cool for a couple of minutes before removing to wire racks. Enjoy!

Mixed Berry Hand Pies

Prep time: 5 minutes | Cook time: 30 minutes | Serves 4

150 g granulated sugar
½ teaspoon ground cinnamon
1 tablespoon cornflour
150 g blueberries
150 g blackberries
150 g raspberries, divided into

two equal portions
1 teaspoon water
1 package refrigerated
shortcrust pastry (or your own
homemade pastry)
1 egg, beaten

Combine the sugar, cinnamon, and cornstarch in a small saucepan. Add the blueberries, blackberries, and ½ of the raspberries. Toss the berries gently to coat them evenly. Add the teaspoon of water to the saucepan and turn the stovetop on to medium-high heat, stirring occasionally. Once the berries break down, release their juice, and start to simmer (about 5 minutes), simmer for another couple of minutes and then transfer the mixture to a bowl, stir in the remaining ½ of the raspberries and let it cool. Preheat the Ninja Foodi Multi-cooker to 190ºC. Cut the pie dough into four 5-inch circles and four 6-inch circles. Spread the 6-inch circles on a flat surface. Divide the berry filling between all four circles. Brush the perimeter of the dough circles with a little water. Place the 5-inch circles on top of the filling and press the perimeter of the dough circles together to seal. Roll the edges of the bottom circle up over the top circle to make a crust around the filling. Press a fork around the crust to make decorative indentations and to seal the crust shut. Brush the pies with egg wash and sprinkle a little sugar on top. Poke a small hole in the center of each pie with a paring knife to vent the dough. Air crisp two pies at a time. Brush or spray the cook & crisp basket with oil and place the pies into the basket. Air crisp for 9 minutes. Turn the pies over and air crisp for another 6 minutes. Serve warm or at room temperature.

Old-Fashioned Fudge Pie

Prep time: 15 minutes | Cook time: 25 to 30 minutes | Serves 8

300 g granulated sugar
40 g unsweetened cocoa
powder
70 g self-raising flour
3 large eggs, unbeaten

12 tablespoons unsalted butter,
melted
1½ teaspoons vanilla extract
1 (9-inch) unbaked piecrust
30 g icing sugar (optional)

In a medium bowl, stir together the sugar, cocoa powder, and flour. Stir in the eggs and melted butter. Stir in the vanilla. Preheat the Ninja Foodi Multi-cooker to 175ºC. Pour the chocolate filing into the crust. Cook for 25 to 30 minutes, stirring every 10 minutes, until a knife inserted into the middle comes out clean. Let sit for 5 minutes before dusting with icing sugar (if using) to serve.

Molten Chocolate Almond Cakes

Prep time: 5 minutes | Cook time: 13 minutes | Serves 3

Butter and flour for the
ramekins
110 g bittersweet chocolate,
chopped
110 gunsalted butter
2 eggs
2 egg yolks
50 g granulated sugar
½ teaspoon pure vanilla extract,

or almond extract
1 tablespoon plain flour
3 tablespoons ground almonds
8 to 12 semisweet chocolate
discs (or 4 chunks of chocolate)
Cocoa powder or icing sugar,
for dusting
Toasted almonds, coarsely
chopped

Butter and flour three (170 g) ramekins. (Butter the ramekins and then coat the butter with flour by shaking it around in the ramekin and dumping out any excess.) Melt the chocolate and butter together, either in the microwave or in a double boiler. In a separate bowl, beat the eggs, egg yolks and sugar together until light and smooth. Add the vanilla extract. Whisk the chocolate mixture into the egg mixture. Stir in the flour and ground almonds. Preheat the Ninja Foodi Multi-cooker to 165ºC. Transfer the batter carefully to the buttered ramekins, filling halfway. Place two or three chocolate discs in the center of the batter and then fill the ramekins to ½-inch below the top with the remaining batter. Place the ramekins into the cook & crisp basket and air crisp for 13 minutes. The sides of the cake should be set, but the centers should be slightly soft. Remove the ramekins from the Ninja Foodi Multi-cooker and let the cakes sit for 5 minutes. (If you'd like the cake a little less molten, air crisp for 14 minutes and let the cakes sit for 4 minutes.) Run a butter knife around the edge of the ramekins and invert the cakes onto a plate. Lift the ramekin off the plate slowly and carefully so that the cake doesn't break. Dust with cocoa powder or icing sugar and serve with a scoop of ice cream and some coarsely chopped toasted almonds.

Glazed Pumpkin Bundt Cake

Prep time: 7 minutes | Cook time: 35 minutes | Serves 12

Cake:
720 ml blanched almond flour
1 teaspoon bicarbonate of soda
½ teaspoon fine sea salt
2 teaspoons ground cinnamon
1 teaspoon ground nutmeg
1 teaspoon ginger powder
¼ teaspoon ground cloves
6 large eggs
480 ml pumpkin purée

240 ml sweetener
60 ml unsalted butter (or coconut oil for dairy-free), softened
Glaze:
240 ml unsalted butter (or coconut oil for dairy-free), melted
120 ml sweetener

In a large bowl, stir together the almond flour, bicarbonate of soda, salt, and spices. In another large bowl, add the eggs, pumpkin, sweetener, and butter and stir until smooth. Pour the wet ingredients into the dry ingredients and stir well. Grease a 1.5 L Bundt pan. Pour the batter into the prepared pan and cover with a paper towel and then with aluminium foil. Place a trivet in the bottom of the Ninja Foodi Multi-cooker and pour in 480 ml of cold water. Place the Bundt pan on the trivet. Lock the lid. Set the cooking time for 35 minutes at High Pressure. When the timer beeps, use a natural pressure release for 10 minutes. Carefully remove the lid. Let the cake cool in the pot for 10 minutes before removing. While the cake is cooling, make the glaze: In a small bowl, mix the butter and sweetener together. Spoon the glaze over the warm cake. Allow to cool for 5 minutes before slicing and serving.

Coconut Almond Cream Cake

Prep time: 10 minutes | Cook time: 40 minutes | Serves 8

Nonstick cooking spray
240 ml almond flour
120 ml unsweetened desiccated coconut
80 ml sweetener

1 teaspoon baking powder
1 teaspoon apple pie spice
2 eggs, lightly whisked
60 ml unsalted butter, melted
120 ml heavy (whipping) cream

Grease a 6-inch round cake pan with the cooking spray. In a medium bowl, mix together the almond flour, coconut, sweetener, baking powder, and apple pie spice. Add the eggs, then the butter, then the cream, mixing well after each addition. Pour the batter into the pan and cover with aluminium foil. Pour 480 ml of water into the inner cooking pot of the Ninja Foodi Multi-cooker, then place a trivet in the pot. Place the pan on the trivet. Lock the lid into place. Adjust the pressure to High. Cook for 40 minutes. When the cooking is complete, let the pressure release naturally for 10 minutes, then quick-release any remaining pressure. Unlock the lid. Carefully take out the pan and let it cool for 15 to 20 minutes. Invert the cake onto a plate. Sprinkle with desiccated coconut, almond slices, or granulated sweetener, if desired, and serve.

Ricotta Lemon Poppy Seed Cake

Prep time: 10 minutes | Cook time: 55 minutes | Serves 4

Unsalted butter, at room temperature
110 g almond flour
100 g granulated sugar
3 large eggs
55 g heavy cream
60 g full-fat ricotta cheese

55 g coconut oil, melted
2 tablespoons poppy seeds
1 teaspoon baking powder
1 teaspoon pure lemon extract
Grated zest and juice of 1 lemon, plus more zest for garnish

Generously butter a baking pan. Line the bottom of the pan with baking paper cut to fit. In a large bowl, combine the almond flour, sugar, eggs, cream, ricotta, coconut oil, poppy seeds, baking powder, lemon extract, lemon zest, and lemon juice. Beat with a hand mixer on medium speed, until well blended and fluffy. Pour the batter into the prepared pan. Cover the pan tightly with aluminum foil. Set the pan in the cook & crisp basket. Set the Ninja Foodi Multi-cooker to 165°C and cook for 45 minutes. Remove the foil and cook for 10 to 15 minutes more, until a knife (do not use a toothpick) inserted into the center of the cake comes out clean. Let the cake cool in the pan on a wire rack for 10 minutes. Remove the cake from pan and let it cool on the rack for 15 minutes before slicing. Top with additional lemon zest, slice and serve.

Vanilla Crème Brûlée

Prep time: 7 minutes | Cook time: 9 minutes | Serves 4

240 ml double cream (or full-fat coconut milk for dairy-free)
2 large egg yolks
2 tablespoons sweetener, or more to taste
Seeds scraped from ½ vanilla

bean (about 8 inches long), or 1 teaspoon vanilla extract
240 ml cold water
4 teaspoons sweetener, for topping

Heat the cream in a pan over medium-high heat until hot, about 2 minutes. Place the egg yolks, sweetener, and vanilla seeds in a blender and blend until smooth. While the blender is running, slowly pour in the hot cream. Taste and adjust the sweetness to your liking. Scoop the mixture into four ramekins with a spatula. Cover the ramekins with aluminium foil. Add the water to the Ninja Foodi Multi-cooker and insert a trivet. Place the ramekins on the trivet. Lock the lid. Set the cooking time for 7 minutes at High Pressure. When the timer beeps, perform a quick pressure release. Carefully remove the lid. Keep the ramekins covered with the foil and place in the refrigerator for about 2 hours until completely chilled. Sprinkle 1 teaspoon of sweetener on top of each crème brûlée. Use the oven broiler to melt the sweetener. Allow the topping to cool in the fridge for 5 minutes before serving.

Crustless Creamy Berry Cheesecake

Prep time: 10 minutes | Cook time: 40 minutes | Serves 12

450 g cream cheese, softened	2 eggs
240 ml granulated sweetener	480 ml water
60 ml sour cream	60 ml blackberries and
2 teaspoons vanilla extract	strawberries, for topping

In large bowl, beat cream cheese and sweetener until smooth. Add sour cream, vanilla, and eggs and gently fold until combined. Pour batter into 7-inch springform pan. Gently shake or tap pan on counter to remove air bubbles and level batter. Cover top of pan with tinfoil. Pour water into Ninja Foodi Multi-cooker and place steam rack in pot. Carefully lower pan into pot. Press the Cake button and press the Adjust button to set heat to More. Set time for 40 minutes. When timer beeps, allow a full natural release. Using sling, carefully lift pan from Ninja Foodi Multi-cooker and allow to cool completely before refrigerating. Place strawberries and blackberries on top of cheesecake and serve.

Apple Dutch Baby

Prep time: 30 minutes | Cook time: 16 minutes | Serves 2 to 3

Batter:	Apples:
2 large eggs	2 tablespoon butter
30 g plain flour	4 tablespoons granulated sugar
¼ teaspoon baking powder	¼ teaspoon ground cinnamon
1½ teaspoons granulated sugar	¼ teaspoon ground nutmeg
Pinch kosher, or coarse sea salt	1 small tart apple (such as
120 ml whole milk	Granny Smith), peeled, cored,
1 tablespoon butter, melted	and sliced
½ teaspoon pure vanilla extract	Vanilla ice cream (optional), for
¼ teaspoon ground nutmeg	serving

For the batter: In a medium bowl, combine the eggs, flour, baking powder, sugar, and salt. Whisk lightly. While whisking continuously, slowly pour in the milk. Whisk in the melted butter, vanilla, and nutmeg. Let the batter stand for 30 minutes. (You can also cover and refrigerate overnight.) For the apples: Place the butter in a baking pan. Place the pan in the cook & crisp basket. Set the Ninja Foodi Multi-cooker to 205°C and cook for 2 minutes. In a small bowl, combine 2 tablespoons of the sugar with the cinnamon and nutmeg and stir until well combined. When the pan is hot and the butter is melted, brush some butter up the sides of the pan. Sprinkle the spiced sugar mixture over the butter. Arrange the apple slices in the pan in a single layer and sprinkle the remaining 2 tablespoons sugar over the apples. Keep the Ninja Foodi Multi-cooker at 205°C and cook for a further 2 minutes, or until the mixture bubbles. Gently pour the batter over the apples. Set the Ninja Foodi Multi-cooker to 175°C cooking for 12 minutes, or until the pancake is golden brown around the edges, the center is cooked through, and a toothpick emerges clean. Serve immediately with ice cream, if desired.

Pumpkin Pie Spice Pots De Crème

Prep time: 5 minutes | Cook time: 7 minutes | Serves 4

480 ml double cream (or full-fat coconut milk for dairy-free)	2 teaspoons pumpkin pie spice
4 large egg yolks	1 teaspoon vanilla extract
60 ml sweetener, or more to taste	Pinch of fine sea salt
	240 ml cold water

Heat the cream in a pan over medium-high heat until hot, about 2 minutes. Place the remaining ingredients except the water in a medium bowl and stir until smooth. Slowly pour in the hot cream while stirring. Taste and adjust the sweetness to your liking. Scoop the mixture into four ramekins with a spatula. Cover the ramekins with aluminium foil. Place a trivet in the Ninja Foodi Multi-cooker and pour in the water. Place the ramekins on the trivet. Lock the lid. Set the cooking time for 5 minutes at High Pressure. When the timer beeps, use a quick pressure release. Carefully remove the lid. Remove the foil and set the foil aside. Let the pots de crème cool for 15 minutes. Cover the ramekins with the foil again and place in the refrigerator to chill completely, about 2 hours. Serve.

Greek Yoghurt Strawberry Pops

Prep time: 5 minutes | Cook time: 0 minutes | Serves 6

2 ripe bananas, peeled, cut into ½-inch pieces, and frozen	yoghurt
120 ml plain 2 percent Greek	240 ml chopped fresh strawberries

In a food processor, combine the bananas and yoghurt and process at high speed for 2 minutes, until mostly smooth (it's okay if a few small chunks remain). Scrape down the sides of the bowl, add the strawberries, and process for 1 minute, until smooth. Divide the mixture evenly among six ice-pop molds. Tap each mold on a countertop a few times to get rid of any air pockets, then place an ice-pop stick into each mold and transfer the molds to the freezer. Freeze for at least 4 hours, or until frozen solid. To unmold each ice pop, run it under cold running water for 5 seconds, taking care not to get water inside the mold, then remove the ice pop from the mold. Eat the ice pops right away or store in a ziplock plastic freezer bag in the freezer for up to 2 months.

Vanilla Pound Cake

Prep time: 10 minutes | Cook time: 25 minutes | Serves 6

110 g blanched finely ground almond flour	1 teaspoon baking powder
55 g salted butter, melted	120 ml full-fat sour cream
100 g granulated sweetener	30 g full-fat cream cheese, softened
1 teaspoon vanilla extract	2 large eggs

In a large bowl, mix almond flour, butter, and sweetener. Add in vanilla, baking powder, sour cream, and cream cheese and mix until well combined. Add eggs and mix. Pour batter into a round baking pan. Place pan into the cook & crisp basket. Adjust the temperature to 148°C and bake for 25 minutes. When the cake is done, a toothpick inserted in center will come out clean. The center should not feel wet. Allow it to cool completely, or the cake will crumble when moved.

Vanilla Butter Curd

Prep time: 5 minutes | Cook time: 6 hours | Serves 3

4 egg yolks, whisked	120 ml organic almond milk
2 tablespoon butter	1 teaspoon vanilla extract
1 tablespoon sweetener	

Set the Ninja Foodi Multi-cooker to Sauté mode and when the "Hot" is displayed, add butter. Melt the butter but not boil it and add whisked egg yolks, almond milk, and vanilla extract. Add sweetener. Whisk the mixture. Cook the meal on Low for 6 hours.

Nutmeg Cupcakes

Prep time: 5 minutes | Cook time: 30 minutes | Serves 7

Cake:	Frosting:
480 ml blanched almond flour	110 g full-fat cream cheese, softened
2 tablespoons grass-fed butter, softened	4 tablespoons grass-fed butter, softened
2 eggs	480 ml heavy whipping cream
120 ml unsweetened almond milk	1 teaspoon vanilla extract
120 ml sweetener, or more to taste	120 ml sweetener, or more to taste
½ teaspoon ground nutmeg	6 tablespoons sugar-free chocolate chips (optional)
½ teaspoon baking powder	

Pour 240 ml of filtered water into the inner pot of the Ninja Foodi Multi-cooker, then insert the trivet. In a large bowl, combine the flour, butter, eggs, almond milk, sweetener, nutmeg, and baking powder. Mix thoroughly. Working in batches if needed, transfer this mixture into a well-greased, Ninja Foodi Multi-cooker-friendly muffin (or egg bites) mold. Place the molds onto the trivet, and cover loosely with aluminium foil. Close the lid, set the pressure release to Sealing. Set the Ninja Foodi Multi-cooker to 30 minutes on High Pressure, and let cook. While you wait, in a large bowl, combine the cream cheese, butter, whipping cream, vanilla, sweetener, and chocolate chips. Use an electric hand mixer until you achieve a light and fluffy texture. Place frosting in refrigerator. Once the cupcakes are cooked, let the pressure release naturally, for about 10 minutes. Then, switch the pressure release to Venting. Open the Ninja Foodi Multi-cooker, and remove the food. Let cool, top each cupcake evenly with a scoop of frosting.

Berry Crumble

Prep time: 10 minutes | Cook time: 15 minutes | Serves 4

For the Filling:	20 g rolled oats
300 g mixed berries	1 tablespoon granulated sugar
2 tablespoons sugar	2 tablespoons cold unsalted
1 tablespoon cornflour	butter, cut into small cubes
1 tablespoon fresh lemon juice	Whipped cream or ice cream
For the Topping:	(optional)
30 g plain flour	

Preheat the Ninja Foodi Multi-cooker to 205°C. For the filling: In a round baking pan, gently mix the berries, sugar, cornflour, and lemon juice until thoroughly combined. For the topping: In a small bowl, combine the flour, oats, and sugar. Stir the butter into the flour mixture until the mixture has the consistency of breadcrumbs. Sprinkle the topping over the berries. Put the pan in the cook & crisp basket and air crisp for 15 minutes. Let cool for 5 minutes on a wire rack. Serve topped with whipped cream or ice cream, if desired.

Mixed Berries with Pecan Streusel Topping

Prep time: 5 minutes | Cook time: 17 minutes | Serves 3

75 g mixed berries	2 tablespoons chopped walnuts
Cooking spray	3 tablespoons granulated sweetener
Topping:	
1 egg, beaten	2 tablespoons cold salted butter, cut into pieces
3 tablespoons almonds, slivered	
3 tablespoons chopped pecans	½ teaspoon ground cinnamon

Preheat the Ninja Foodi Multi-cooker to 170°C. Lightly spray a baking dish with cooking spray. Make the topping: In a medium bowl, stir together the beaten egg, nuts, sweetener, butter, and cinnamon until well blended. Put the mixed berries in the bottom of the baking dish and spread the topping over the top. Bake in the preheated Ninja Foodi Multi-cooker for 17 minutes, or until the fruit is bubbly and topping is golden brown. Allow to cool for 5 to 10 minutes before serving.

Coconut Lemon Squares

Prep time: 5 minutes | Cook time: 40 minutes | Serves 5 to 6

3 eggs

2 tablespoons grass-fed butter, softened

120 ml full-fat coconut milk

½ teaspoon baking powder

½ teaspoon vanilla extract

120 ml sweetener, or more to taste

60 ml lemon juice

240 ml blanched almond flour

In a large bowl, mix together the eggs, butter, coconut milk, baking powder, vanilla, sweetener, lemon juice, and flour. Stir thoroughly, until a perfectly even mixture is obtained. Next, pour 240 ml filtered water into the Ninja Foodi Multi-cooker, and insert the trivet. Transfer the mixture from the bowl into a well-greased, Ninja Foodi Multi-cooker-friendly pan (or dish). Using a sling if desired, place the dish onto the trivet, and cover loosely with aluminium foil. Close the lid, set the pressure release to Sealing. Set the Ninja Foodi Multi-cooker to 40 minutes on High Pressure, and let cook. Once cooked, let the pressure naturally disperse from the Ninja Foodi Multi-cooker for about 10 minutes, then carefully switch the pressure release to Venting. Open the Ninja Foodi Multi-cooker, and remove the dish. Let cool, cut into 6 squares, serve, and enjoy!

Printed in Great Britain
by Amazon